The Complete Family Guide to College Financial Aid

The Complete Family Guide to College Financial Aid

Richard Black

A PERIGEE BOOK

A Perigee Book
Published by The Berkley Publishing Group
200 Madison Avenue
New York, NY 10016

Book design by Irving Perkins Associates

Cover design by Wendy Bass

First edition: October 1995

Published simultaneously in Canada.

Library of Congress Cataloging-in-Publication Data

Black, Richard W.
    The complete family guide to college financial aid / Richard W.
Black. — 1st ed.
        p.   cm.
    "A Perigee book."
    ISBN 0-399-52158-5 (pbk. : alk. paper)
    1. Student aid—United States—Handbooks, manuals, etc.
    2. Student loan funds—United States—Handbooks, manuals, etc.
    3. Scholarships—United States—Handbooks, manuals, etc.   I. Title.
    LB2337.4.B53   1995
    378.3′0973—dc20   95-8201

Printed in the United States of America

10 9 8 7 6 5 4 3 2 1

This book is printed on acid-free paper.

To my mother, Helen Black Humbarger, and my father, John Wilson Black, who planned for my education; and to every trustee, politician, taxpayer and philanthropist who has supported a financial aid program.

A Disclaimer and a Note on Costs, Contributions and Other Dollar Values

I have carefully researched this book so that the information will be as accurate as possible at the time of publication. However, *The Complete Family Guide to College Financial Aid* cannot always be accurate for the unique circumstances of each student, each post-secondary educational institution and each financial aid program, nor can it refer to the inevitable changes which will occur. In general the costs, contributions and other dollar values are accurate as of the 1994–95 academic year, but some data or concepts may be inaccurate, and dollar values will change in succeeding years. Neither the author nor the publisher can be responsible for errors of that sort in this book. Use the guide to make general plans, then follow the specific instructions appropriate for your circumstances from the financial aid program or the individual educational institution.

Contents

PART C
SPECIAL CATEGORIES OF STUDENTS

Introduction

The '90s are an exciting time for financial aid for higher education. No longer do parents who own a home find it difficult to receive financial aid. Congress has authorized loan programs for all parents of college students. There are even loan programs for students who can't demonstrate that they need student aid. The '90s are also a challenging time because now, more than ever in our history, Americans need some kind of postsecondary education to succeed, or just survive.

I believe parents have to be guides, and they need guidebooks. This is a guidebook on college financial aid. It defines the scholarship, grant, loan and employment programs and leads the reader through the application process. Some of us started with Dr. Spock, or maybe a Lamaze handbook. This book is for parents who want to know about financial aid for their unique student, whether that student is headed for a highly selective college, a community college, or a one-year trade school program. It offers advice for students applying for athletic scholarships, students with disabilities, and students planning for graduate or professional school.

This is a also a guidebook for another group of parents—those who want to be students, including teen-age mothers and moms and dads who are in their mid-twenties to mid-forties. These people need education beyond high school today so they can earn more or even hold on to the jobs they have. They need postsecondary education to set an example for their kids, to catch up with their kids, or just to make life more meaningful.

College costs a lot, but it's a good investment. For decades, the incomes of people who graduate from college have been higher than those who have only a high-school education. In the last five years, studies have shown that persons with a college education are less likely to be unemployed, and when they do lose their jobs, they get new positions more quickly than workers without a college education. Consequently, it's financially rewarding for parents to guide children toward college, and for them to complete their own higher education. While I will emphasize the financial rewards of higher education in this guide, another powerful incentive is personal growth and fulfillment. Conceivably you won't undertake more education for the financial rewards; your motivation could be personal fulfillment, a deeper understanding of an area, or self-improvement. These motivations are just as legitimate as the financial rewards of advanced study, and for many people more powerful.

Finally, this book offers advice about financial aid for study after college. Such study might include a professional school, such as law school or medical school; it could be for a Ph.D. in graduate school in the sciences and the arts, or it could be for a master's degree in fields such as education, public administration, health administration, library science or other specialized fields.

I speak from 30 years of experience in financial aid. I also speak as a parent of a private college Phi Beta Kappa graduate, a Berkeley grad who is in medical school, a high-school senior who looks like he might be an engineer, and a ninth-grader who excels in athletics and music. My wife has a master's degree in public administration that she financed from current income, and my employer paid for my graduate study through a tuition remission program. So this little book is what I've learned in theory and what I've learned through practice. I think parents will find it useful.

The Complete Family Guide to College Financial Aid

Part A
How Financial Aid Works

Read this part to learn the basics of financial aid

This is a book about how to get financial aid, but I don't discuss the financial aid programs until page 20. It's okay with me if you skip ahead to learn about the individual programs, and then come back to learn how you qualify. However, I counsel a little patience. Let's talk about costs, parent contribution and student contribution, and need. Most financial aid is awarded through the following formula: **cost** minus **parent contribution** minus **student contribution** equals **need,** which is met with a **financial aid package**. That is, need is met with some combination of scholarship, grant, loan and work. Got it? Good. Let's make it the first rule and then talk about college costs.

RICH BLACK'S RULE #1.
Cost minus parent contribution minus student contribution equals need.

1

Costs

Lots of parents start their consideration of colleges by looking at the costs. Everyone knows that college tuition is high. But how much is it? Is tuition of $1,300 a year high? That's the average tuition of a community college in the United States. It's also about equal the $110 a month that many teenagers spend on entertainment and gas for a car. Is $2,700 a year high? That's the average in-state tuition of a state university today. Is $12,000 a year a lot? That's a typical tuition for a moderately selective independent college or university. Is $20,000 a year high? Yes, but many families pay it to send their children to Ivy League and other highly selective universities.

So much for my four questions. Let's look at the costs of three different kinds of colleges, and then let's examine the difference between living at home and living away at college. First, the following table lists the expenses other than tuition and fees that every student who does not live with parents must pay. These costs are accurate for the 1994–95 academic year.

These numbers will change somewhat depending on the location of the college. Some rural and southern colleges tend to cost less. Some urban, East Coast, and West Coast colleges cost more. The range could be as much as $1,000 either way. However,

Expenses in Addition to Tuition

Item	Per Year
Housing, Utilities and Food (Room and Board)	$5,760
Books and Supplies	648
Personal	1,566
Transportation	738
Total, excluding tuition and fees	**$8,622**

RICH BLACK'S RULE #2.
Most of the difference in the student's total cost of education is the cost of tuition. Costs for room and board are surprisingly uniform at public or private colleges.

students will pay these costs whether they go to a public community college, a public university, or a private college. $8,620 is still a good chunk of change. Is there any way to reduce it? Sure; the easiest way is to live at home, assuming there is a college that meets your needs within commuting distance. The California Student Aid Commission reports the following costs for students living with their parents.

Annual Average Costs for California Students Living with Parents

Item	Per Year
Housing, Utilities and Food (Room and Board)	$2,196
Books and Supplies	648
Personal	1,620
Transportation	594
Total, excluding tuition and fees	**$5,058**

Presumably most of the $2,196 listed for room and board is for meals on campus. For some parents, the difference between the $8,622 and the $5,058 is critical. These parents may also feel the student should live at home for a few more years. For others, the $3,564 increased cost of living away from home is an important investment in the student's independent living skills. They note that students who reside on campus associate with new college friends, make informal contacts with older students and faculty, and have more opportunity to participate in campus activities such as athletics, drama, community service and student leadership.

RICH BLACK'S RULE #3.
Students can reduce total educational costs by as much as $3,600 if they live at home. Balance this savings against lost educational opportunities.

Now, about tuition and fees. There are several factors that influence these costs. Is the college tax-supported, and therefore a public college? Is it tuition-supported, or a private, independent college? Is it a trade or technical school? If so, it can be either tax- or tuition-supported. If the college is tax-supported, how much more does it charge for out-of-state students? Is the private college highly selective and therefore likely to be more costly? Or is it less selective and likely to be more moderate in cost? The cost of tuition and fees at some typical colleges and universities are listed on the next table.

It's easy to spend more on extra entertainment, clothes, automobiles, travel and other expenses. But some students do it for less by living in co-operative houses where they share in the maintenance or the cooking, by renting the less expensive rooms in residence halls such as a triple that three students share, or by attending college in a part of the country where expenses are lower. These costs will give a basis for planning.

Total Annual Student Costs to Attend Six Representative Institutions, 1994–95

Name	Type	Cost In-State	Cost Out of State
Stanford University, Palo Alto, CA	Highly Selective, Independent	$28,000	$28,000
Loyola University of Chicago, IL	Selective, Independent	$20,000	$20,000
Ohio State University, Columbus, OH	Selective, Major Public	$11,000	$17,000
San Francisco State, San Francisco, CA	Less Selective, Public	$10,000	$17,000
Community College of Denver, Denver, CO	Open Door Community College, Public	$10,000	$16,000
DeVry Institute, Chicago, IL	Vocational College, Private, For Profit	$14,000	$14,000

2

Parent Contribution

Here comes the hard part—at least if you are a parent. But before you get too depressed, remember the student contribution is still to come, and it can be significant. And remember too, many parents don't cover the whole cost from current income; they save for college before the actual event, and they borrow for college, and repay after graduation. And one more thing: there are some savings when the student leaves the house. The food bill goes down a little, and the utility bill goes down a little, and the car insurance bill can go down a lot if you can remove the teen-age driver from your policy. So some funds can be freed up for college expenses.

And, fellow parents, this hard part just got easier! You know how you have been reading for years that if you owned a house you couldn't get financial aid? Well, home equity did increase parental contribution before the fall of '93. But since that time, home equity has no longer been counted in determining federal financial aid!

RICH BLACK'S RULE #4.
Recent changes in need analysis rules, particularly the exclusion of home equity, have made it easier for students to qualify for need-based financial aid.

Now, how is parents' contribution calculated? The federal methodology for need analysis is similar to the federal income tax calculations, which is not too surprising since the U.S. Congress approves both. If your income is low, say less than $25,000, the federal need analysis methodology requires you to contribute little or nothing toward the cost of a child's higher education. As your income rises, the methodology requires you to contribute more.

If you are determined to understand every detail of need analysis, you need to get a copy of the "Counselor's Handbook for Postsecondary Schools" published by the U.S. Department of Education, Student Financial Assistance Programs. The simplest thing to do is borrow the financial aid officer's copy at a local college. Please return it, because it's her Bible.

Your contribution is not necessarily expected from current income. You may make the contribution from savings or loans. The table below incorporates several important factors upon which parent contribution is based: parent income, assets, and number of family members in college. (Your assets are cash, savings, checking accounts and investments.) To get a rough idea of your parent contribution, find the income and number of family members in college that approximates your situation. If your assets are higher than $40,000, your parent contribution may increase by $600 for each $10,000 of assets. If your family has more than four members, your parent contribution will be lower.

"Ye dogs and little pups!" you say. How do they possibly expect

Expected Parent Contribution for a Family of Four, with One or Two Family Members in College, Assets of $20,000 at Four Different Income Levels

Name	Parental Income	Parent Contribution, 1 in College	Parent Contribution, 2 in College
Jason	$20,000	$ 0	$ 0
Daisy	$40,000	$ 4,000	$2,000
Alexander	$60,000	$ 8,000	$4,000
Maria	$80,000	$14,000	$7,500

me to come up with $4,000, or $8,000, or $14,000? Well, some parents can do it with good financial planning. These are the parents who began to save for their child's education when the student was born. Or maybe they bought mutual funds over the years. Or they bought life insurance that has built up a cash value. It's never too late to start saving. If it's October of your child's senior year in high school, start making those monthly payments to a savings account now. It will give you just that much of a start on making the first loan payment, or postpone the time you must take out a loan, thereby reducing the interest you must pay.

Let me tell you how my friend Mrs. Lee did it. Daisy's mother is self-employed as an insurance agent with a modest business in our neighborhood. She is also a single parent. The summer before Daisy entered the eighth grade, Mrs. Lee realized she would need to contribute $4,000 a year when Daisy got to college. She reasoned that saving is better than borrowing. So she planned to invest $67 a month in a money market mutual fund. By the time Daisy's first bill for her freshman year came due, five years later, she calculated she would have $4,020, plus the interest she had earned. That extra interest might cover the increase in college cost during the five-year period.

However, Mrs. Lee realized that Daisy had more than one year to pay for. She had four years! So before Daisy's high school freshman year she increased her savings to $134 a month, before her sophomore year she saved $201 a month and before her junior year she saved $268 a month. Again in Daisy's senior year Mrs. Lee had to save $268 a month. Then she gave a gentle sigh as the required savings went down in the college freshman year to $201, further down in the sophomore year to $134, and all the way back down to $67 during Daisy's junior year. The table Mrs. Lee used to plan her "eighth-grade-thru-college-eight-year-investment-program" is at the top of the next page.

Now, Mrs. Lee had another option. She could have simply waited until the beginning of Daisy's senior year in high school, and begun to save then. Had she done that, she would have had to save $333 a month in order to make the $4000 payments at the beginning of each college year.

Monthly Savings for $4000 Parent Contribution for Four Years of College

	Year In High School					Year In College			
	8	9	10	11	12	Fr.	Soph.	Jr.	Total
Monthly Savings									
For Freshman Year	$67	$ 67	$ 67	$ 67	$ 67				$4,020
For Sophomore Year		$ 67	$ 67	$ 67	$ 67	$ 67			$4,020
For Junior Year			$ 67	$ 67	$ 67	$ 67	$ 67		$4,020
For Senior Year				$ 67	$ 67	$ 67	$ 67	$67	$4,020
Total Each Month	**$67**	**$134**	**$201**	**$268**	**$268**	**$201**	**$134**	**$67**	

The following table shows how Alex's parents and Maria's parents could use the "eight-year-investment-program" approach for their parent contributions. Under this approach, Alex's parents must contribute $8,000, and thus if they begin when he enters the eighth grade, they will need to save $133 a month to begin with, and $532 a month during the maximum savings period of Alex's junior and senior years of high school. If they try to save it all starting in Alex's senior year of high school, they must save $667 a month. In comparison, Maria's father and mother can consider saving $1,166 each month for four years, or stair-step up and down from $233 to $933 to $233 if they start five years before Maria goes to college.

Maria's father, Mr. Lopez, a lawyer with a practice at the county seat, saw that the eight-year program would not work for him.

Savings Required for Parent Contributions at Three Income Levels

Name	Parent Contribution Per Year	Level Payment (Save for 12 Months Before Academic Year)	Minimum Payments (Save for 60 Months Before Each Academic Year)	Maximum Payments During Last 2 Years of High School
Daisy	$ 4,000	$ 333	$ 67	$268
Alex	$ 8,000	$ 667	$133	$532
Maria	$14,000	$1,166	$233	$933

There was no way he could save $933 a month, which would be his maximum payment for a $14,000 annual expense. Therefore, he took Mrs. Lee's approach one step farther. He too started saving when Maria began the eighth grade, but in addition he took out a loan with a five-year repayment term at the beginning of each of Maria's four years in college. So he saved for five years before college, and then he borrowed at the beginning of each college year to make up for the rest of the parent contribution that he had not saved. He paid off each loan over a five-year period.

He contributed $14,000 for Maria's freshman year in college from savings and from a loan. To meet this expense he invested $117 a month, which totaled $7,020 plus interest by the time Maria was ready to start her freshman year. Then he borrowed the remaining $6,980, which he repaid over the next five years. His monthly payments were more than $117 because he had to pay 8% interest on his loan, but I have omitted the interest for purposes of simplicity. Mr. Lopez's savings stair-stepped up each year just like the eight-year plan we discussed above, but his plan is really a 13-year plan. In the eighth grade he invested $117 a month; by the eleventh grade his savings were $468, where they stayed until the end of the first year after college at which time they began to reduce. Mr. Lopez's 13-year program of saving and borrowing is illustrated below and on the next page. The **bold** figures on the table represent repayment of loan principal. Actual payments would be higher because of interest.

A 13-year Program of Saving and Borrowing for Education

	Year In Junior High and High School					Year In College			
	8	9	10	11	12	Fr	So	Jr	Sr
Monthly Amount For Freshman Year	$117	$117	$117	$117	$117	**$117**	**$117**	**$117**	**$117**
For Sophomore Year		$117	$117	$117	$117	$117	**$117**	**$117**	**$117**
For Junior Year			$117	$117	$117	$117	$117	**$117**	**$117**
For Senior Year				$117	$117	$117	$117	$117	**$117**
Month Total	**$117**	**$234**	**$351**	**$468**	**$468**	**$468**	**$468**	**$468**	**$468**

Year After College				
1	**2**	**3**	**4**	**Total**
$117				$14,000
$117	$117			$14,000
$117	$117	$117		$14,000
$117	$117	$117	$117	$14,000
$468	$351	$234	$117	

Next, let's assume that Mr. Lopez had the best of intentions, but he never got started on his savings program. "Pomp and Circumstance" is still ringing in his ears from high-school graduation, and he must borrow the $14,000 each year. He can get a home equity loan for 8% and choose to pay it off in 10 years. What will his payments be? His stair-steps will last over 13 years. They will begin at $146 and get as high as $595 for years four through ten, at which point they will step back down to $146 in year thirteen. Because he did not plan ahead, his payments will be $146 to $595 rather than $117 to $468.

Before being too harsh on Mr. Lopez for not investing from the eighth grade, I note that borrowing for college may actually make more sense for some parents than investing ahead of time. Parents' income may continue to rise during or after their children's college years, and therefore loans may be easier to repay than investments were to make. Perhaps there are other events in a family's financial history, such as an anticipated inheritance, or going from one parental wage earner to two wage earners when the student goes off to college, which make loans more reasonable—or less necessary—than savings. Each family will manage these expenses differently. The parent contributions are a major lifetime expense, right up there with a house, retirement and major medical emergencies, but parents manage them by saving, by making monthly payments, and by borrowing.

RICH BLACK'S RULE #5.
Parents provide the parent contribution through some combination of monthly savings before college, monthly payments during college and loan payments after college.

This discussion has focused on parent contribution and assumed that there will be one family member in college, but look back to the table on page eight. Notice that the parent contribution for two family members in college is half that of families with one in college, and I could have added a third column to show that families with three family members in college cut the contribution in thirds. Many parents with children close together in age despair when they see the parent contribution for the first child going off to college, reasoning that the contribution for the second child who will be entering college in the second year will cause them to double their contribution. In fact, the contribution stays approximately the same, and is spread over the two children—or three children—or however many family members are in college.

Did you notice I said family members? What if mom goes back to college? Does she get a "parent contribution"? She sure does. Most institutions using the federal need analysis methodology count mom and dad right in there if they will attend at least half-time for at least one term. Some independent colleges don't allow parents to be counted as students under all circumstances when they award their own funds, but even they will make some allowance against parent contribution. A thirst for knowledge is a wonderful thing, and if a parent was planning on gaining a next degree anyway, sometimes the best time is when the kids go off to college.

RICH BLACK'S RULE #6.
Parent contribution is divided by the number of family members in postsecondary education. Get two for the price of one.

3

Student Contribution

Student contribution is a lot easier to calculate than parent contribution, because most students have a simpler financial situation than most parents. The federal need analysis methodology takes what the student earned in the previous calendar year after taxes, then subtracts a $1,750 "income protection allowance" and multiplies the remainder by 50%. To that add 35% of the student's assets and *voilà!,* you have the student contribution.

Let's take Daisy as an example: her 1993 earnings were $2,000 and her assets on the date of application were $2,000, so what is her student contribution for 1994–95?

1	1993 Taxable Income	$2,000
2	Minus $1,750 Income Protection Allowance	−1,750
3	Available Income	250
4	Times .50 for Income Contribution	125
5	Student Assets	$2,000
6	Times .35 for Asset Contribution	700
7	**Total Student Contribution (Lines 4 + 6)**	**$ 825**

So let's look at the four students we have been discussing so far, and see what their student contribution for study in 1994–95 would be.

Student Contributions for Four Hypothetical Students

Name	1993 Earnings After Taxes	Assets on Date of Application	Student Contribution
Jason	$5,000	$ 0	$1,625
Daisy	$2,000	$ 2000	$ 825
Alex	$1,000	$ 0	$ 0
Maria	$1,500	$10,000	$3,500

What produced the income and assets that effected the contributions in each case? Jason had worked a lot in 1993, perhaps because his parents had an income of $20,000 and the family needed Jason's income to meet basic family expenses. The theory is that if he earned it before he applied for financial aid, he can still earn some of it before being awarded financial aid. Therefore he is still expected to come up with $1,375 on his own before any financial aid will be awarded. ($5,000–$1,750) × .50 = $1,625. I don't agree with the theory in this case and advise Jason to appeal; procedures for appeals are discussed below.

Daisy is expected to give almost nothing from her earnings. The $2,000 she earned generates a contribution of $125 once the $1,750 is subtracted. Most of her contribution comes from the 35% of the $2,000, or $700, that she has in the bank. Alex needs to make no contribution because he earned less than $1,750 and has nothing in the bank. Maria has a lot of money in the bank because her grandmother gave it to her for college. And her contribution from those savings is high: $10,000 × .35 = $3,500. Grandmother could have maximized Maria's eligibility for financial aid by just paying a part of Maria's bill each year. High student assets generate high student contributions.

I commend students who work while they are in high school to help their parents, to pay their own expenses, or to save for college. But I have a responsibility to explain how student earnings and assets affect financial aid eligibility as calculated by the federal methodology. Students who earn over $1,750 or have significant assets are expected to make a contribution to the financial cost of their education. To maximize financial need, and financial aid to meet that need, keep earnings and student assets down.

RICH BLACK'S RULE #7.
Student contributions are calculated from previous year's income in excess of $1,750 and 35% of student assets. A student with income in excess of $1,750 a year will reduce eligibility for aid.

4

Need

The concept underlying calculating need for financial aid is straightforward. Cost, minus parent contribution, minus student contribution, equals need for financial aid. The four tables that follow present the need calculations for the four students we have been discussing: Jason, Daisy, Alex and Maria. You may remember from the table on page 8 that these illustrations assume one family member in college and $20,000 of assets other than the family home.

Need Calculation for Jason
(Parental Income $20,000 or Less)

	Stanford	Ohio State	Community College of Denver	De Vry Institute
Cost	$28,000	$11,000	$10,000	$14,000
Parent Contribution	0	0	0	0
Student Contribution	1,625	1,625	1,625	1,625
Need	$26,375	$ 9,375	$ 8,375	$12,375

Obviously Jason will need a major financial aid package to attend whatever college he chooses. The problem for Jason's parents will not be the contribution they make to his college expenses. It will be doing without the funds he contributed to the household while he was in high school. His college expenses are so high, even at the community college, that he will not be able to assist his family.

Need Calculation for Daisy (Parental Income $40,000)

	Stanford	Ohio State	Community College of Denver	De Vry Institute
Cost	$28,000	$11,000	$10,000	$14,000
Parent Contribution	4,000	4,000	4,000	4,000
Student Contribution	825	825	825	825
Need	$23,175	$ 6,175	$ 5,175	$ 9,175

Daisy will have financial need wherever she goes. If she goes to the community college, she can limit the amount she must borrow.

Need Calculation for Alex (Parental Income $60,000)

	Stanford	Ohio State	Community College of Denver	De Vry Institute
Cost	$28,000	$11,000	$10,000	$14,000
Parent Contribution	8,000	8,000	8,000	8,000
Student Contribution	0	0	0	0
Need	$20,000	$ 3,000	$ 2,000	$ 6,000

Alex has little need at the community college, because his $8,000 parent contribution is just $2,000 less than the $10,000 cost of attendance. He will need more aid at the state university and the technical college, and he has a large need at the highly selective private college.

Need Calculation for Maria (Parental Income $80,000)

	Stanford	Ohio State	Community College of Denver	De Vry Institute
Cost	$28,000	$11,000	$10,000	$14,000
Parent Contribution	14,000	14,000	14,000	14,000
Student Contribution	3,500	3,500	3,500	3,500
Need	$10,500	$ 0	$ 0	$ 0

Maria needs $10,500 in aid, which is a lot of money, if she wishes to attend the highly selective college. Otherwise her parent contribution and her student contribution are sufficient to pay for her education. Remember that Maria's student contribution comes from her $10,000 in assets. If she works and borrows, she can increase the amount she can contribute and reduce the amount her parents must provide.

Incidentally, the illustrations above show each student receiving in-state tuition in Ohio and Colorado, a logical impossibility since a student can reside in only one state at once. To see what out-of-state costs would be add $7,000 to Ohio State and $6,000 to Community College of Denver. But be careful! Many public colleges do not meet full need for out-of-state students. Read the financial aid offer letter carefully to be sure these additional costs are covered by the financial aid package.

Some families go for low cost to keep need and parent contribution low. Some families think the more expensive schools are worth it because financial aid meets need, and the prestige of the degree may be greater. You'll have to make that judgement yourself, but wait until you understand the financial aid programs before you make up your mind.

5

The Financial Aid Programs: Federal, State, Institutional and Private

THE TYPES OF FINANCIAL AID

Gift Aid

Scholarships are gift aid offered on the basis of excellence.

Grants are gift aid offered on the basis of need.

RICH BLACK'S RULE #8.
Scholarships and grants are gift aid, which is the best kind of aid because it doesn't have to be earned or repaid.

Self-Help Aid

Loans are financial aid that must be repaid. Most loan programs are designed to be repaid by the student, although some are for parents. Sometimes the borrower must pay the interest while in school, but in the best programs the government pays the interest while the student is in college. Sure as graduation follows registration, loans come due, and then there can be a rude shock. How much will your payments be? Many educational loans are 10-year notes and have minimum payments of $50 a month. Most borrowers will pay more than the minimum. I estimate that payments for the 10-year notes are $13 a month for each $1000 borrowed, if interest is 8% or 9%. A student who borrows $10,000 will owe $130 a month for 10 years. Is it worth it? Think carefully about this question; I ask it several times throughout this book. On the one hand, borrowing money to get an education that will increase your earning power makes a lot of sense. On the other hand, accumulating payments that are more than you can afford to repay will lead to a poor credit rating, which will degrade rather than increase the quality of your life. Poor credit is a bummer.

RICH BLACK'S RULE #9.
Estimate your loan payments by rounding the total amount borrowed up to the nearest thousand. Multiply $13 by the number of thousands to determine your monthly payments. Borrow for education what you can expect to repay from increased earnings. If your monthly payment is more than you can afford on what you expect to earn, then seek less costly education.

My $13 rule may become obsolete as a whole new set of repayment options become available through the Direct Loan Program. The rules for these options are still being written, and no one has used them yet because the first Direct Loans are going into repayment as this book is published, but by the time students reading this book go into repayment, millions of students could be taking advantage of them. Therefore I provide a short discussion of these options in the Appendix. Each of these options provides a mechanism for lower monthly payment, although in most cases the student will pay more interest over the long run then he or she would have with the 10-year repayment rules.

In addition, many organizations that service student loans will arrange temporarily reduced payments to assist students through periods of reduced income. If you find yourself getting behind in loan payments, contact your loan servicer, discuss your financial situation and see if you can arrange for lower payments.

Student employment is work that the student undertakes while attending a college or university. Students often work full-time during summer vacations and part-time during the academic year, but there are many variations. The Federal College Work Study Program (often called just "work study") is a popular federal program in which a portion of a student's wage is paid by a federal grant, and a portion paid by an on-campus or off-campus, usually nonprofit, employer. Since a federal grant pays part of the student's wage, students with work-study eligibility usually get first crack at on-campus jobs. The debates on working your way through school are endless. There are two basic positions: (1) I did it and I don't want my kid to do it; and (2) Working won't hurt anything. In fact, this is an area that's been studied a lot. All the studies say the same thing: 10 hours a week or less for freshmen won't hurt grades, and 15 hours a week for upperclassmen won't hurt grades. Anything beyond that will have some effect on grades.

How much can a student earn? Assume a pay rate of $6.50 an hour. A student who works 40 hours a week for 10 weeks in the summer can earn $2,600, and would take home at least $2,000. A student who works 15 hours a week during the academic year for 32 weeks would earn $3,120 and take home about $2,500. So a student could realistically provide $4,500 toward college expenses from earnings. Notice that we have accounted for only 42 weeks, so our $4,500 earnings assumption still leaves 10 weeks a year for exams, vacations and other times when employment is not possible.

RICH BLACK'S RULE #10.
Most students can work up to 15 hours a week during the academic year without adversely affecting academic achievement.

FINANCIAL AID FROM THE FEDERAL GOVERNMENT

Grant Programs

The **Federal Pell Grant Program**: Awards up to $2,300 for low-income students.

The **Federal Supplemental Educational Opportunity Grants**: Awards up to $4,000 for low-income students.

Loan Programs

The **Federal Stafford Student Loans:** Loans of $2,625 for freshmen, $3,500 for sophomores and $5,500 for juniors and seniors. Graduate students can borrow $8,500 a year. Repayment of principal and interest begins after the student ceases college education. These loans are made by banks and other lenders with administrative support from intermediary guarantee agencies and financial oversight by the U.S. Department of Education.

The **Federal Unsubsidized Stafford Loans:** Same conditions as the Federal Stafford Student Loans, except students need not demonstrate financial need. Student borrowers must pay the interest while they are in college. These loans also are made by banks with guarantee agency support and Department of Education oversight.

The **Federal Perkins Student Loans:** Loans of up to $3,000 a year for undergraduate study and $5,000 a year for graduate study. These loans are made by the colleges and universities themselves with funds acquired largely from repayments by alumni. The funds that established this program over the last 35 years were 90% federal funds and 10% institutional funds.

The **Federal PLUS Loans:** Loans for parents that do not require financial need but do require that the parents be credit-worthy. Repayment begins immediately. Parents may borrow the full cost of a student's education, less any financial aid the student receives. These loans, like the Stafford Loans, are made by banks with Department of Education and guarantee agency support.

The **Federal Direct Loan Programs:** Parallel programs to the above bank loan programs that are administered by the colleges

themselves and the Department of Education. Five percent of all student loans in 1994–95 were made by colleges and universities, which then sent the loans directly to a federal contractor who collects deferment forms, bills the student, and does the other tasks needed to service a student loan. Because the college or university is disbursing the loan, the time between the award letter and the disbursement of the loan should be much shorter. The federal government expects to save some money through Direct Lending, since it won't be subsidizing banks to make these loans. Therefore, it will increase Direct Lending to 40% of all loans in 1995–96 and more in subsequent years. In 1997 Congress will evaluate the progress of Direct Lending and decide whether to phase out the bank loans entirely, continue with both Direct Loans and bank loans, or go back to the present system where the banks make the loans. The official names of these programs are: The **Ford Direct Student Loans;**
The **Ford Direct Unsubsidized Loans;** and
The **Ford Direct PLUS Loans**.

From the borrower's point of view, the terms of the loans are virtually identical; the only difference is that the promissory note comes from the college instead of the lender.

Work Programs   The **Federal College Work-Study Program:** A student employment program in which a federal grant provides a major share of the student's wage, and an on-campus or off-campus employer pays the remainder of the student's wage.

FINANCIAL AID FROM THE STATE

Many states offer grant programs. For instance, California offers the "**Cal Grant A**" program, a need- and merit-based program that provides up to $5,600 a year to attend an independent institution, up to $3,799 to attend a campus of the University of California, and up to $1,450 to attend a campus of the California State University System. It also offers the "**Cal Grant B**" program, a need-based program for the neediest students. In addition to the payment of fees, the program also pays for room and board.

Many other states and the District of Columbia offer grants and scholarships to residents. Check with your local high school guidance counselor or the reference room in your library for the grants in your state.

FINANCIAL AID FROM THE INSTITUTION ITSELF

Colleges and universities are one of the largest providers of grant and scholarship aid. They employ a major proportion of their students with their own funds, and many colleges sponsor loan funds. When you apply for financial aid, you will be considered for the college's assistance along with the federal and state financial aid programs.

FINANCIAL AID FROM PRIVATE AGENCIES

The list of private scholarship programs fills entire directories. This list includes PTA's, the National Merit Scholarship Foundation, the Elks, and scholarships sponsored by employers for children of employees. It includes community scholarship foundations and prestigious national scholarship organizations such as the Harry Truman Scholarship Foundation as well as literally thousands of local scholarship assistance agencies. Most private scholarship programs have a separate application. Many require separate essays and interviews. The best source for information on these scholarships is books in the library. Lately some high-school guidance offices have installed computers that help identify these scholarships. Encourage your student to spend some time searching these databases for scholarships for which he or she is eligible. Part C of this book introduces Max, an industrious chap who successfully applied for outside scholarships.

RICH BLACK'S RULE #11.
A financial aid package is a combination of scholarship, grant, loan and employment awards funded by the federal government, the state government, the colleges themselves and outside agencies.

6

The Application Process

How do you apply for financial aid? You just file the FAFSA. Say what? The FAFSA—The Free Application for Federal Student Aid. This remarkable document, which is used for institutional and state financial aid programs in addition to the federal programs, becomes available late in the calendar year in high-school guidance counselor offices and university financial aid offices all across the country. March 1 is the filing deadline at many selective colleges, but some colleges may want the form even earlier. Some may let you file it later. So get the form in January and carefully review college application materials to determine colleges' application deadlines. Completing this form will allow you to have your financial information sent to up to six colleges and universities. It allows you to be considered for all of the federal financial aid that institution awards. Many colleges, universities, state scholarship agencies and other scholarship organizations also use it for their own financial aid. So it's a good deal.

It's also a pain to complete. Most parents prefer to have their tax forms handy when they complete it, *ALTHOUGH THAT IS NOT REQUIRED*. You can estimate the parental income, or you can do your taxes early so you have accurate data for the FAFSA, and then set the tax forms aside till April 14. Here are a couple of essential FAFSA rules:

1. Read the instructions. If it says fill it out in pencil, use a pencil. If it says use a pen, use a pen. Follow all the other instructions. Don't leave any items blank.
2. File the FAFSA by the deadline.

Sounds simple, huh? Well, the schedule doesn't accommodate delays. This data is run through the federal servicer's computers in early March, the college's computers in early April, and then appears on the financial aid offer letters in mid-April. Students must make their admissions deposits by May 1. This schedule allows no time for colleges and universities to write back and help you correct errors. Why should it matter whether or not you use a pencil or a pen? It matters because this is a complex financial aid delivery system that serves over 6 million students, but it sure works better for those who take a little extra time and care to follow the instructions.

Some colleges or scholarship programs may want other forms. Many institutions want you to complete and submit a Financial Aid Form (FAF) along with the FAFSA. This form requests additional information that colleges need to award their own funds. If the college or university wants this form, it will tell you in its instructions. Use the same care in completing this form that you used with the FAFSA.

Make copies of everything you send off! This is important for two reasons:

1. You have to fill out these forms every year the student wants financial aid, so having last year's form will help you next year; and
2. Sometimes the various processors, colleges and awarding agencies lose the forms. Should that happen, you may need to send in your copies.

When you mail the forms, you may want to get proof of mailing. Do not send these forms by certified or registered mail. That slows down the process because someone must personally sign for the letter. But there is a procedure called "Certificate of Mailing" which now costs 55 cents. Use that procedure, and keep the slip you get from the post office, plus your copies of the forms. The receipt and the copies of the forms will often be enough to allow whatever office lost or misfiled your forms to acknowledge that you did your part on time and accept your application as being submitted before the deadline.

About three weeks after you file the FAFSA, you will receive a Student Aid Report, or a SAR, from the federal processor. This document will repeat all of the data you submitted on the FAFSA, and ask you if it is correct. If data is incorrect, either because you gave incorrect data or because the processor entered it incorrectly, you are to enter the correct data and send it back to the processor. If the data are correct, you should sign the form and send it to the college you will attend. Some colleges have a different procedure, and if they do they will inform you accordingly.

The FAFSA, the SAR, and possibly the FAF, are just the beginning. There will be loan forms, employment forms, lots more forms. Remember to copy them before you send them in also. But the FAFSA, and the FAF if you require it, will get you started.

RICH BLACK'S RULE #12.
Get the FAFSA and the other forms well before the deadline and complete them carefully, reading the instructions when you have any questions. Make copies of every form you mail, and file before every deadline.

7

Financial Aid Award Packages
for Dependent Students

What is a financial aid "package"? It's a combination of grant, scholarship, loan and work that meets a student's need. It would be great, of course, if we could give every needy student enough scholarship and grant aid to meet his or her need. But there isn't enough grant money to do that. And some people feel it isn't justified to meet all the need with scholarships and grants. They argue that since the student gets so much benefit from a college education, the student should pay for some of the cost of education through loans and through work. So out of necessity, morality or both, we add loan and work, which in combination with grant and scholarship aid meets the need for most students.

Let's look at some tables for the students we have discussed so far to illustrate the concept. I will introduce several hypothetical institutions, "Prestige Private University," "Major State University," "Career Institute" and "County Community College" to illustrate financial aid packages, since most universities do not publish their packaging policies the same way that they publish their costs. Please do not assume that Stanford, Ohio State, Community College of Denver and DeVry Institute offer these packages, because I am not familiar with the packaging policies at those institutions.

Financial Aid Packages for Four Students at Major State University ($11,000 Budget)

Name & income	Family Contribution*	Calculated Need	Scholarship or Grant	Loan	Work
Jason $20,000	$ 1,625	$9,375	$4,375	$2,500	$2,500
Daisy $40,000	$ 4,825	$6,175	$1,175	$2,500	$2,500
Alex $60,000	$ 8,000	$3,000	$ 0	$1,000	$2,000
Maria $80,000	$17,500	$ 0	$ 0	$ 0	$ 0

* The "family contribution" is the parent contribution added to the student contribution.

Several comments are helpful in understanding this table. First, we have assumed that the cost at Major State University is $11,000 a year. The family contribution subtracted from the budget determines the student's need. The last three columns outline the financial aid package that the student receives to meet his or her financial need.

Jason's parent contribution was zero and his student contribution was $1,375, so his family contribution was $1,375. Subtract the family contribution from the cost and the need is $9,625. His package meets his need. His scholarship and grant award probably comes from several different sources; he may have a federal Pell Grant for $2,300 and a state grant for $2,075. He must still earn $2,500 from a job during the academic year, save it from a summer job, or do both. And he must borrow $2,500 during the academic year.

Daisy has a lower need because her parent contribution is higher. She still receives some scholarship aid, perhaps from her state scholarship agency or perhaps from Major State itself. She has the same loan and work expectations that Jason had.

Alex's need is much lower because his parent contribution is higher. He still has some loan and work expectation. Alex could apply for a scholarship from a private agency—that is, from an agency other than the federal government, the state government or the institution itself. There might be a scholarship offered by a parent's employer, a PTA, a local community service group such as the Elks, or even the National Merit Scholarship Foundation. Major State, and many colleges and universities, allow these scholarships to replace loan and work before they reduce their own institutional scholarships. Thus, if Alex received a scholarship for $1,000 for his entry in the local science fair, this award would reduce the amount he had to earn or borrow.

Maria, on the other hand, has a parent contribution of $14,000. Since that exceeds the cost of a Major State education, Maria has no eligibility for need-based financial aid. If she wins the PTA scholarship for $1,000, she and her parents will certainly breathe a sigh of relief. Maria has another option. She can work just as Jason, Daisy and Alex do. She can earn $3,000 and reduce the parent contribution to $11,000. Or her parents can provide the $14,000, and Maria can use the $3,000 she earns for extra expenses, like a trip to Florida for spring break or a trip to New Orleans for Major State's appearance in the NCAA basketball tournament Final Four. She might use the $3,000 to buy a computer work station on which she can design circuit boards or choreograph ballet. Maria has more economic options open than Jason.

Now that we see how financial aid packages work at Major State, let's look at them for students at Prestige Private University, Career Institute and County Community College.

Look at the packages on the next two pages. They represent the amazing variety and complicated financial picture that confront American high-school seniors. At Prestige Private University each student has financial need. The students earn and borrow about the same. Prestige Private uses its own funds to make large grant awards to many students. At the other end of the cost scale is County Community College, where most students don't have to earn or borrow much if their parents make the parent contribution. Even if their parents don't make the full contribution, most students can earn and borrow enough to support themselves. Students at Major State University and Career Institute are somewhere in between these two extremes.

Financial Aid Packages for Four Students at Prestige Private University ($28,000 Budget)

Name & Income	Family Contribution	Calculated Need	Scholarship or Grant	Loan	Work
Jason $20,000	$ 1,625	$26,375	$18,875	$4,500	$3,000
Daisy $40,000	$ 4,825	$23,175	$15,675	$4,500	$3,000
Alex $60,000	$ 8,000	$20,000	$12,500	$4,500	$3,000
Maria $80,000	$17,500	$10,500	$ 3,000	$4,500	$3,000

Financial Aid Packages for Four Students at Career Institute ($14,000 Budget)

Name & Income	Family Contribution	Calculated Need	Scholarship or Grant	Loan	Work
Jason $20,000	$ 1,625	$12,375	$2,300	$4,750	$5,325
Daisy $40,000	$ 4,825	$ 9,175	$ 0	$5,000	$4,175
Alex $60,000	$ 8,000	$ 6,000	$ 0	$3,000	$3,000
Maria $80,000	$17,500	$ 0	$ 0	$ 0	$ 0

Financial Aid Packages for Four Students at County Community College [$10,000 Budget]

Name & Income	Family Contribution	Calculated Need	Scholarship or Grant	Loan	Work
Jason $20,000	$ 1,625	$8,375	$2,300	$3,000	$3,075
Daisy $40,000	$ 4,825	$5,175	$ 0	$ 0	$ 0
Alex $60,000	$ 8,000	$2,000	$ 0	$ 0	$ 0
Maria $80,000	$17,500	$ 0	$ 0	$ 0	$ 0

These packages may not represent those offered by the colleges your child might attend. It may be that a college wants special talents that your student has. So while the aid will not exceed need, the college may offer grant or scholarship assistance instead of loan and work assistance. You won't know what the college will do until your child gets his financial aid offer letter. That's an excellent reason for applying to as many as six different colleges.

RICH BLACK'S RULE #13.
Colleges meet financial need with a financial aid package, which is a combination of scholarship, grant, work and loan. Colleges differ in the amount of scholarship and grant in the package, so compare packages carefully.

8

Responding to Verification

Again and again I hear comments like the following: "Those people down the street have a Mercedes and a BMW and their kid gets a scholarship, while all you will give us is a loan. It's not fair and you should stop helping them or give us more!" From the late '50s, when colleges and the federal government began to develop the current financial aid programs, there have been efforts to verify the information that students and parents submit so that funds are distributed equitably and so that scarce funds are not allocated without justification. At first these efforts were somewhat subjective, with aid officers collecting information about cars and boats or assessing home equity by zip code.

From these rather subjective beginnings evolved a federally regulated process called verification, based on the examination of parents' and student's federal income tax forms as well as other information that could document a student's eligibility or need. Federal financial aid regulations require that financial aid offices examine income tax forms from at least 30% of the applicants. Many colleges and universities require that all applicants and the parents of dependent students submit copies of tax forms filed, including all schedules.

As a consequence of verification, many students and parents choose to file the FAFSA after they have filed their tax forms. Certainly this makes it much easier to report consistent numbers. However, the tax deadline is April 15 and the college or university may request a FAFSA as early as February 15. When that happens, financial aid applicants have no choice but to file the FAFSA with estimated data, and then correct the data if the estimates prove to be inaccurate later.

Financial aid offices may request a plethora of additional documents, and the following list is not exhaustive:

Immigration documents
Proof of marriage
Birth certificates
The Financial Aid Transfer Record from previous colleges
Divorce records and other family legal records
Proof of sibling enrollment in another college or university

Providing this additional documentation can be a time-consuming and frustrating experience for student, parent and financial aid office administrative personnel; but the verification requirements are absolute. If one of these documents is missing from a folder, auditors can disallow the entire financial aid award, which could require the student or the college to repay everything received. Obviously neither the college nor the student or parent can afford such an outcome, so students and parents must provide the documents and financial aid offices must file them.

RICH BLACK'S RULE #14.
All colleges will require tax forms and other supplemental documents from at least some of their applicants. Follow the instructions of the colleges to which you apply. Make copies of every form submitted and meet every deadline.

MULTIPLE AWARD LETTERS

Don't be surprised if you get a succession of revised award letters. Some financial aid offices send out preliminary award letters, which give only an approximation of the financial aid available until verification is completed. Then again, you may receive a final or official award letter, only to receive a second and third revised official award letter when outside funding agencies provide the financial aid office with information about the aid that they are providing you.

To help you understand why financial aid offices can't seem to get it right the first time, I have to introduce the concept of an "overaward." The federal government can't afford to award a student more in grants, loans or work-study employment than he or she needs. So when a student receives an award from a state grant agency or an outside scholarship agency, in addition to the financial package that has already been offered the student, the financial aid office must reduce one of the student's other awards. Usually the reduction is in loan or employment, one of the less desirable forms of financial aid. Such a reduction maintains the student's incentive to seek scholarships from organizations other than the college or university. But if the reduction in loan or employment is not sufficient to compensate for the additional aid, the college may reduce its own grant aid to prevent an overaward. Some financial aid offices simply reduce their own grant aid so they can award grant funds to some other student.

RICH BLACK'S RULE #15.
Be prepared for a succession of offer letters, understand the change that each represents, sign and return them as the instructions will provide, and appeal if you think it's appropriate.

9

Filing an Appeal

"There must be some mistake. They couldn't possibly expect us—or my parents—or me . . . to contribute what this letter says we are to contribute. How can we appeal?" Fully a third of financial aid applicants must appeal some aspect of the calculated family contribution or the financial aid package. These appeals can involve the parent contribution, the student contribution from income and assets, the unique expenses that a particular student must pay, or the composition of the financial aid package itself. What constitutes grounds for a successful appeal and which appeals are likely to be granted?

A successful appeal has three parts: (1) It states that the financial aid decision is based on incorrect or incomplete information; (2) It is carefully documented; and (3) It is persistently addressed. Success is less likely when the appeal is couched in vague or emotional language. The appeal is almost always resolved at the institution's financial aid office. The central need analysis processors are in Iowa, New Jersey, or Washington, D.C., and they may have toll-free phone numbers for questions about whether or not forms have been received or processed, or perhaps what number was used in a particular calculation. If your appeal involves more than a simple data entry error, the financial aid office will have to make it.

Many financial aid offices have standard forms for appeals. Find out from the financial aid office of the college in question how they accept appeals, and follow those instructions. It's probably best not to think of your appeal as an adversarial situation. You have your financial constraints, and the financial aid office has to follow federal, state, institutional and funding agency regulations. Hopefully the financial aid office can reconcile your constraints and the funding agency regulations. But when it has reviewed matters thoroughly, if it has not given all the aid you had hoped for, that is probably the end of the matter. Of course, you can appeal to your elected representative, the chief executive officer of the college or the university, and in certain cases to boards established to assure student rights. The effect of such appeals is to make the financial aid office explain its procedures to a third party, and that can be useful. Be prepared, however, for an outcome other than the one you want, and make your educational plans accordingly. Appeals are such an important activity a second section on the topic is given in Part C-7 later in this book.

Here are some common appeals and the documentation you may be asked to provide:

Condition	Documentation
Loss of Parental Employment	Layoff notice, unemployment compensation papers
Additional Parental Expense	Bills and receipts for medical expenses, additional support for relatives, and other nondiscretionary expenses
Additional Student Expense	Bills and receipts for medical expenses, essential educational supplies, and other nondiscretionary expenses
Loan Default Reported	Proof that you were enrolled in college or met some other condition so that no payments were due. Or, proof that you made payments.

RICH BLACK'S RULE #16.
File an appeal that is factual with supporting documentation. Use the college's appeal forms if any are appropriate.

10

The Second Year and Beyond

After you have done everything the first year, you have to do it all over again for every subsequent year: another FAFSA, another round of award letters, and another round of appeals if you need to make them. Don't miss the deadlines! Every year I have to inform sophomores that they didn't apply on time for their second year, and therefore they don't get the same financial aid package they got for the first year.

College costs will go up each year, or at least they have for the last 30 years I have been in the business, because the expenses that students and colleges must pay go up. Room and board increase, faculty salaries increase, the costs of books for the library and oil for the classroom furnaces increase. Hopefully financial aid funds will go up as well, although in recent years loan funds have increased faster than grant and scholarship funds. So, there are changes constantly surging through the financial aid process that make it unlikely the financial aid in a student's second year will be the same as in the first year.

Many colleges and universities will keep the financial aid package in the second year and beyond as similar to that in the first year as they can. Thus, if costs go up $1,000 from the freshman to the sophomore year, the institution will increase self-help by $500 and grant assistance by $500. But your individual package may not reflect this at all. For one thing, your own circumstances may have changed. If a second parent becomes employed in the student's sophomore year, then the parent contribution will increase dramatically, and the financial aid will decrease just as dramatically. If the student has a scholarship that requires a 3.0 average, and the student has a 2.8 for the freshman year, then the scholarship will be gone in the second year. If the stock market plunges and the value of the institution's investment portfolio shrinks, there may be less money for scholarships in the later year. Finally, some institutions choose to give students more grant money in the first year, and then replace grants with loans and work in the second year and beyond either because they feel that students in their first year can work and borrow less, or as a deliberate marketing strategy.

What should a parent or a student do when confronted with this reality? For the first year, it's well to be aware that changes could come in the second year and beyond. If the financial aid package is barely adequate for the freshman year, perhaps it's prudent to look at another college or university where the package is a bit more affordable. On the other hand, most institutions are ethical and do not give students and parents major changes in their financial aid in upperclass years unless the family's circumstances have changed, because they are committed to supporting the student through to a degree.

RICH BLACK'S RULE #17.
Apply for financial aid each year. Assume that the financial aid will be somewhat different in the upperclass years, but adequate to support the student through to graduation.

At various places throughout the book, I give a timeline that you can use as a checklist. I hope you will read the entire book, or at least scan it for relevant sections. Then come back to the sections that most apply to you. When you have completed a task, check it off and give yourself a pat on the back. Financing a college education is tough work, and you deserve some credit for keeping on schedule. Then move on to the next task. I hope these checklists help keep you on schedule as you move toward your educational goals.

The Timeline and the Checklist

What	When	Done?
Start a regular monthly savings plan. What you don't save, you will have to borrow.	At birth of child? While student in jr. high? As soon as possible	
Fill out the FAFSA to get an idea of your expected family contribution.	Sophomore year of high school	
Take a look at colleges. What are their costs?	Junior year of high school	
List college application deadlines and meet them. After January 1—but before college deadline—fill out FAFSA and college financial aid forms.	Senior year of high school	
Read financial aid offer letters from colleges that admit student. How much grant and scholarship? How much loan and work? Help your student choose best college or university for him or her.	Senior year of high school	
Fill out supplemental forms that financial aid office will provide. Make payments when they are due.	April, senior year of high school	
Miss the deadlines? Apply late and appeal. Some programs take applications until three weeks before the end of the school term.	April to fall registration	
Meet the same financial aid application deadlines as for the first year.	Second year and beyond	

Part B
Parents as Students

Read this if you are a parent going on, or back, to college

1

Financial Aid for Parents as Students

The previous section of *The Complete Family Guide to College Financial Aid*, Part A, frequently assumed the perspective of the parents who needed to guide a teen-ager through the financial aid process. This section, Part B, is intended for an entirely different group of students—those who are parents themselves! I'll call them "parent students." The American Council on Education reports that 40% of today's college students are "non-traditional," a group composed of older students, students attending part-time, and students who have dependents. Virtually none of these parent students can count on their own parents for financial support for college, and they have the joys and responsibilities of parenthood themselves. Some have a spouse to help them. Some do not. Most are twenty-something, but then again some are in their teens, some are in their 30's and a growing number find college begins after 40. The overwhelming number come to college to qualify for those better employment opportunities now available only to those with education beyond the high-school level.

U.S. News & World Report reported on eighteen growing employment fields, from tax accounting to telecommunications manager. Fifteen of these fields required at least a bachelor's degree. Parent students face challenges to fulfill their ambitions: they have to get the kids to day care, get the dinner on the table and then get their studies done. They meet these challenges with stamina, discipline and determination. If you have the choice, get the degrees before you get the family. But a degree is more worthwhile for the additional support it can provide a family. A substantial portion of American college students—perhaps 3 million of the brightest people in this country—are parenting and going to college. If they can do it, so can you. Get any grant you can get, work as much as you can, and then borrow what you need. Big deal if it takes you six and a half years to finish a four-year degree; big deal if you come out owing $10,000 in student loans. For most people an under-graduate degree adds the opportunity to get a new job or a promo-tion worth hundreds of dollars a month. Those hundreds of dollars will pay off the loan while they enhance your standard of living, and when the loans are paid off, you'll have a lot more discretion-ary money. And besides, you'll be a better role model for the kids.

RICH BLACK'S RULE #18.
40% of American college students can't be wrong. Financial aid—along with the student's own earnings—can make a college degree a reality. That degree will make you a better provider for your kids, and a better role model for them as well.

INDEPENDENT STUDENT STATUS

Now that we see the financial aid that supports millions of parent students, let's review the financial aid basics. If you have read Part A, you'll recognize the concept we discussed there: **COST MINUS PARENT CONTRIBUTION MINUS STUDENT CONTRIBUTION EQUALS NEED.** Financial aid officers use this concept for parent students too, but there is no parent contribution. Students who are parents are considered independent by the federal govern-ment's need-analysis methodology. There is no expectation that the parents of these students will contribute toward the cost of the student's higher education. Congress has said you do not need to provide information about your parents' income when applying for federal financial aid if you are at least **one** of the following:

- a parent yourself
- over the age of 24
- a veteran of the armed services
- married
- a foster child or a student whose parents are dead
- a student in graduate school

RICH BLACK'S RULE #19.
If you are a parent, the federal government does not expect your parents to make a contribution toward your education to determine your need for financial aid.

FINANCIAL AID PROGRAMS AND THE APPLICATION PROCESS FOR PARENT STUDENTS

How does financial aid work for students who are parents? Some of the concepts are the same as for the dependent student. If you skipped Part A and came directly to Part B, please read the sections from Part A that begin on the pages indicated before you continue: "How Financial Aid Works"—page 1; "The Financial Aid Programs"—page 20; and "The Application Process"—page 26. If you are anxious to start the application process, you can read the following sections later: "Responding to Verification"—page 34; "Filing an Appeal"—page 37; and "The Second Year and Beyond"—page 39.

Did you read at least the first three sections I listed in the above paragraph? Good, because I'm going to assume you know about the loan programs and the Pell Grant programs. But as a parent student, you need some additional information about these aid programs. Like dependent students, parent students will work and borrow to pay for their education, and many will do both. Loans and employment are the college conundrum—the baffling problem—of the parent student's life. Work too much, and there is no time for the studies and the kids. Borrow too much, and your repayments will exceed the amount your degree will add to your monthly income. Unfortunately, some students borrow more than they can repay, and go into default, which is such a disaster that I discuss it three different times in this book: here for parent students, back on page 21 for dependent students and again on page 130 for graduate students. Each time I discuss the issue, I note that you can estimate your monthly payments by multiplying $13 times the amount you have borrowed in thousands. Thus, if you borrow $10,000, your payments will be 10 times $13, or $130.

Can you afford to make the payments on what you will earn when you graduate? If you default, you will be hassled by collectors, your credit report will reflect the default so you can't borrow for a car or a home, and you will not be able to receive financial aid. But supposing you do default; what then? Call the student loan billing agency that has your loan. It's best if you can do this before you default, but you can call any time. Ask the billing agency what it will require to remove the default status. The agency may ask that you repay all the amount currently due, which is probably not possible. Ask the agency if there are deferments that can be applied retroactively. Sometimes you can remove your loan from default by filing deferments. As a last resort ask the agencies if they will accept monthly payments to restore the loan to an active status, and thus remove your loan from default status.

RICH BLACK'S RULE #20.
Don't default, but if you do, negotiate with your student loan billing agency and resume regular payments. Defaulters lose eligibility for all financial aid, not just loans.

Now, about the Pell Grant Program. It is the federal grant program that most needy parent students can count on for gift aid support. Any parent student qualifies for a Pell Grant who earns less than $12,000 in the calendar year prior to the academic year in which he or she will enroll. For example, for academic year 1995–96, if you earned under $12,000 for 1994 then you qualify for a Pell Grant. Full-time students will receive $2,300, half-time students $1,150, and three-quarter-time students something in between. And if you earned more than $12,000, you may still qualify for some Pell Grant assistance. Most dependent students will attend full-time, and therefore qualify for the maximum grant; but parent students are much more likely to attend less than full-time because they have to take care of their children and work. If you can, go full-time to maximize the Pell Grant and get your degree as soon as possible.

The application process for parent students is the same as that for dependent students. It begins with the completion of the Free Application for Federal Student Assistance (FAFSA) as discussed on page 26, and then continues with the supplemental forms that colleges and financial aid programs will provide. But there's a hitch. The deadlines for these programs are set with the schedules of high-school seniors in mind. Many parent students miss the deadlines because they decide to attend postsecondary education closer to the beginning of the academic term. The payoff to parent students for meeting the deadlines is so significant it deserves a rule.

RICH BLACK'S RULE #21.
Application deadlines are set with high-school seniors in mind. Parent students who meet the deadlines can give themselves substantial financial benefits.

COLLEGE COST AND THE PARENT STUDENT

The basic financial aid equation can be restated for the parent student: **COST MINUS STUDENT CONTRIBUTION EQUALS NEED.** And remember that need is what financial aid officers meet with some combination of grant, loan and work. How do they calculate the student's cost and the student contribution? Parent students frequently disagree with financial aid officers on the answer to this question. For dependent students we learned that the cost of tuition, fees, books and supplies is added to room, board and incidental expenses to come up with the student's budget, or student's cost. So you would think that the student parent's budget would be the same, plus the cost of supporting the children. But federal financial aid regulations do not allow for the basic maintenance of the child or children; they allow only the cost of child care, and sometimes then only with a separate appeal! Therefore, from the beginning the parent student's costs will be at a minimum several thousand dollars higher than the financial aid officer's estimate of cost. Yet don't give up. Just realize that parent students have to recognize two sets of educational costs: the lower ones, which do not include housing and food for the children, and the higher ones, which include these costs.

On the other hand, federal regulations do allow some of the costs of supporting the children to be subtracted from the student's income before expecting any contribution to educational expenses. I will illustrate the parent student's calculation of costs and the financial aid calculation when I discuss Cecile, Amy and several other students, and I'll offer two of my rules in succession to deal with child care and the difference between costs as the financial aid officer calculates them and costs as the student calculates them.

RICH BLACK'S RULE #22.
Child care can be included in the parent student's budget, but often only after filing a separate appeal.

RICH BLACK'S RULE #23.
Parent students can calculate expenses and resources thousands of dollars higher or lower than financial aid officers because they have different assumptions. Therefore look at the financial aid offer letter, then make your own statement of expenses and financial aid. Compare the two and make your decision.

STUDENT CONTRIBUTION FOR PARENT STUDENTS

At the risk of boring you through repetition, I repeat the basic formula: **COST MINUS STUDENT CONTRIBUTION EQUALS NEED.** Let's look at the calculation of "student contribution" in more detail. Like "parent contribution," student contribution for parent students is based on student earnings, student assets, and the expenses that a student faces. Perhaps that is enough detail for you. When you get the Student Aid Report (see page 28) back after you file the FAFSA, you will see how much you are to contribute from each source. If you don't want more detail, skip down to the discussion on "Veteran's Benefits, Employee Benefits and Public Assistance" on page 54. If you are a need-analysis detail freak, get the "Counselor's Handbook for Postsecondary Schools," which I mentioned on page 8.

Student contribution for parent students with incomes in the prior calendar year of less than $12,000 is zero. That's simple, isn't it? A single parent student can make minimum wage for a year and not be expected to contribute anything toward college. It doesn't even matter if she has assets. This is one rule that makes perfect sense. If you earn less than $12,000 a year, or if you and your spouse earn less than $12,000 a year, and you have a child, then there is no way you can have money for college, and the federal government doesn't expect you to provide any.

RICH BLACK'S RULE #24.
If you are a parent, and you and your spouse had a total income of less than $12,000 in the previous year, your student contribution is zero.

I do have to add a caveat. I have to tell you that the "under $12,000" rule applies automatically only if the parent student was eligible to file a federal tax form 1040EZ or 1040A. Trust me, most people who earn under $12,000 don't have to file the 1040, the long form. Most people who file the long form claim deductions for home mortgages, have income over $50,000 and in general have a lot more income or assets than most people who earn $12,000. But if you have some weird financial situation—for example, you had financial accounts in a foreign country in excess of $10,000—then you could have income under $12,000 and not qualify for the simple needs analysis. Okay, so in summary, parent students who earn under $12,000 and can file the 1040EZ or the 1040A form automatically qualify for a student contribution of zero.

Now how about the over-$12,000 parent students? If you add your adjusted gross income (from your tax forms) and that of your spouse to untaxed income such as AFDC and child support, and it is over $12,000, then you will probably have to make a student contribution. To calculate the contribution:

add	adjusted gross income
+	untaxed income
subtract	federal income tax paid
−	Social Security tax paid
−	allowance for state taxes
−	income protection allowance
−	employment expense allowance
equals	available income
times	contribution rate
equals	contribution from income

The terms given above are self-explanatory until you get to the *income protection allowance* and *the employment expense allowance*. What are these? The "income protection allowance" is an allowance for basic living expenses apart from college expenses that the student must pay before contributing to college expenses. The larger the family, the larger the income protection allowance. For two family members, it is $10,840; three family members, $13,490; four family members, $16,670; and so forth. Because these allowances include the cost of supporting the parent student's children, these costs are not included in the educational budget of the student.

Now for the "employment expense allowance." The friendly folks in the Department of Education just think it costs a single parent more to earn a week's wage than a single person with no kids, that's all. Or, if you are married it costs more to earn a given amount when you and your spouse work, because when two parents work both incur clothing, food, and other costs associated with employment.

Let's review the arithmetic. First we calculate "available income," which equals total income, less federal income tax, less Social Security taxes, less state tax allowance, less income protection allowance, less employment expense allowance. And we are going to take a portion of available income (from a table like those used for income taxes) for educational expenses.

Hold on, though. We aren't there yet. (I said you might want to skip all this.) Do we have to figure a contribution from assets? No. Those friendly feds decided that parent students didn't have to make any contribution from assets if their income was under $50,000 and they filed or were eligible to file a 1040A or a 1040EZ. So that keeps it simple. There is a contribution from assets for those with incomes over $50,000, but if you are a parent student with an income over $50,000 all you qualify for is an unsubsidized student loan. See page 23.

Veteran's Benefits, Employee Benefits and Public Assistance

Part A presented the financial aid programs, but for the most part it focused on need-based programs for which a student applied using the FAFSA. Three major programs, which are independent from the need-based financial aid programs, require special discussion: veteran's benefits, employee educational benefits and public assistance.

Veteran's benefit programs provide a range of monthly stipends for education. See section B-4 below. Most financial aid officers will let veteran's benefits replace loan and work, so veteran's benefits supplement any grants a student may receive. Refer to the case of John below for an illustration of how veteran's benefits can be integrated with other financial aid for the parent student.

Employee educational benefits are a magnificent untapped resource for many working parent students. Many employers will pay much or all of a student's tuition for employees. Some require that the courses be work-related and taken on the employee's own time, but many will support any education and will even pay employees to take the courses on company time. Sure, it takes longer to get a degree if you study part-time, but for many parent students a part-time degree is the best option. Tricia, section B-5 below, provides an example of a student gaining her degree with employee benefits.

Public assistance will support some parent students, or at least some of the cost of raising the children, in some areas of the country. Sometimes the support is in medical benefits or food stamps if not in an actual cash stipend. At present, public assistance programs are under renewed scrutiny as a way to reduce government expenditures, and the programs have never been uniform from state to state or even from county to county within a state, so do not assume that because you are a low income parent student you qualify for benefits. But do check out the benefits offered by the counties in which the educational institutions you are considering are located.

YOUR SPOUSE, YOUR MOM AND YOUR DAD

A parent student may or may not have a spouse. Four of the examples that I present below are of single parents; two involve married students. I'm not telling you anything you don't know when I say that a spouse adds economic stability. This is the case if the spouse is working and therefore providing support, and it is usually the case if the spouse is a student and therefore getting his or her own financial aid package. What if you are on your own? Well, child support can still be a big help. While it's true that child support is counted as income on the FAFSA, it's still money that doesn't have to be paid back.

Finally, every parent student should explore one more source: the bank of mom and pop. True, the federal government doesn't require financial assistance from parents of students who are parents themselves, and true, most parents consider that you are on your own when you marry or have a child, but still, you can ask. Many parents of parents will help in a pinch, whether with a tuition payment for a semester, Christmas presents for the kids because you spent the Christmas money on the winter quarter tuition, or a new clutch for the Ford because the old one went out while you were cramming for exams. Interestingly enough, the federal government has no financial aid regulations on such matters. They treat $3,000 from mom and dad like any other source of "other income" and do not assume that because you got it you are a dependent student. You know your folks and what they'll do, but don't forget to ask. The worst they can do is say no.

RICH BLACK'S RULE #25.
Don't forget to ask mom and dad. They might chip in.

I'd like to illustrate the basic financial aid understandings for parent students that I have addressed so far by introducing you to six students who remind me of successful parent students I have known in recent years. Each will hear "Pomp and Circumstance" while marching across the stage with tassel dangling from mortarboard to shake the dean's hand. Each illustrates some different sources of financial support and some unique adaptations to higher education that student parents utilize to realize their dream of a degree. I've listed the four single parents first, and then the two students who have spouses to help them out. The first two students attend community college, the next three a state university and the last an independent college. Read through the illustrations to see which ones have information that could be of help to you.

Name	Illustrates
Cecile	A low-income single mother who has child-care costs. She works part-time and full-time while she studies at a community college. She receives a scholarship from a community organization.
Amy	A low-income mother receiving public assistance for study at a community college.
John	An unemployed father of two with veteran's benefits. Illustrates the details of the calculation of student contribution and an appeal to the aid officer at a state university.
Tricia	Full-time worker using employee benefits. She studies part-time at a state university and uses employee educational benefits.
Simmons and June	Two parent students with two financial aid packages at a major state university.
Sylvia	A student whose spouse has a middle-class job and who studies full-time at an independent university.

2

Cecile

A low-income single mother with child-care costs who works full-time and part-time. She has a scholarship from an outside agency and attends a community college.

Cecile is a 19-year-old single mom with a two-year-old daughter and a high-school diploma. She earned $8,582 at a fast-food restaurant last year and has $500 in the bank. When she told the manager of her restaurant that she wanted the manager's job someday, the manager said she had better get a business degree, and the community college was the place to start.

She sent a postcard to the local community college to get a copy of the Free Application for Federal Student Aid, or FAFSA, the same form used by dependent undergraduates. She completed it, including the code for the local community college, and mailed the FAFSA to the federal processors. (Refer to page 26 for information on the application process.) The results of that form came back in about three weeks on a Student Aid Report, a SAR, which indicated that she was eligible for assistance. She also applied for admission and financial aid at the college.

She made a list of her expenses for a year of study:

Expenses	Amount
Tuition/Fees	$ 1,450
Books	600
Room/Board/Personal	8,200 ($680 a month)
Child Care	2,700
Total	**$12,950**

Cecile lives in Colorado, where typical community college tuition and fees are about $1,450 a year for 12 units a term and $1,750 for 15 units a term. She estimated the cost of books at $600 and room, board and personal expenses at $8,200 a year. That was a rock-bottom budget for her and her daughter, which worked out to about $680 a month. That included $350 a month rent for the apartment she shared with her girl friend and her son, $200 a month for food, and $130 a month for everything else. She knew that's what she lived on, because that is what she took home from her job. In addition she would have her child care costs.

When Cecile got her financial aid offer letter from her college, she compared her estimate of expenses (right column) with the college's estimate (left column). She also compared the financial aid the college offered (left column of second table) and what she eventually received (right column). Look at each line in the following tables, and then I'll explain the significant differences.

	College's Figures	Cecile's Figures
Tuition/Fees	$ 1,450	$ 1,450
Books	600	600
Room/Board/Personal	6,200	8,200
Child Care*	2,700	2,700
Total	$10,950	$12,950
Minus Student Contribution	0	0
Equals Need	$10,950	$12,950

* Granted after appeal to financial aid office.

Financial Aid	Offered	Received/Accepted
Grants	$ 2,300	$ 2,300
Loans	2,625	
Work	5,775	6,600
Other		
Church Scholarship		1,250
Child Support		2,800
Total Financial Aid	**$10,700**	**$12,950**

The first thing Cecile noticed was that her student contribution, at the bottom of the first table, was zero. Cecile meets the $12,000 income ceiling criterion for parent students, so she has no student contribution. The next thing she noticed was that the college's calculation of need was much lower than what she had calculated, and she thought her budget for living was low already! When she asked me about that, I had to say that federal regulations assumed that her income would cover her child's living expenses, including food and rent. However she could—and did—appeal for inclusion of babysitting costs. (See page 64 for appeals.) The financial aid office increased her budget to include these costs, but its total was still $2,000 lower than the costs she calculated.

Then Cecile studied the award the financial aid office had offered. Of course she accepted the grant for $2,300, which was a Pell Grant, but she declined the loan. Some students think they must take the loan and the work offered in a financial aid package to get a grant or a scholarship, but this is not the case. Her financial aid officer told her that her loan would go into repayment if she interrupted her college studies for a couple of semesters. If she did not make the payments on her loan during the semesters when she was not registered for college, her loan would go into default. Then she would not be eligible for any further financial aid, including the Pell Grant. She decided that when she was near the end of her studies, she might borrow, but for the time being it was better to work more and study less rather than take out the student loan.

The $5,775 of work in Cecile's financial aid package could be employment under the Federal College Work Study program. This is a need-based financial aid program in which the employer pays a portion of the wage and the federal government pays the other portion through a grant to the college or university. However, in her case it was simply her job as a waitress at a local chain restaurant. This particular restaurant served breakfast 24 hours a day, so Cecile could almost always schedule hours. In order to earn $6,600 she figured she would have to cut down to 20 hours a week during the academic year, and then work 40 hours a week during the summer and the vacations. That was tough but feasible.

Cecile also applied for and received a special scholarship, in this case one from her church. Although she had to drop out of the choir except at Christmas and Easter because she didn't have time for choir practice, she still qualified for $1,250 a year from the church scholarship fund when she turns in copies of her school bills. (See page 110 for more information on applying for special scholarships.)

Child support really isn't financial aid, but it sure helped Cecile, so I listed it. Her daughter's father would provide child support of $54 a week. Getting him to provide the support took some doing, because Cecile found it hard to talk with him. To his credit, he was really interested in his daughter; and so even though he was a pain, Cecile kept in touch with him.

Now, about studying full-time. If she could go minimum full-time, composed of 12 units a semester, which is three or four classes, she could get a Pell Grant for $2,300. If she went less than full-time, her Pell Grant would be reduced. The full-time Pell Grant would cover tuition, books, and a little more. At 12 units a semester, it would take Cecile five years to get her undergraduate business degree.

In reality it will probably take longer, because there might be semesters when she could not pass 12 credits, but even if it takes six or seven years she would be more employable and better able to support her child with her undergraduate degree than without it.

3

Amy

*A low-income mother receiving public
assistance who attends a community college*

Amy is a single mother with three children, the oldest of whom is
14. After losing her job when a local printing plant closed down,
she began to receive unemployment benefits for herself and public assistance benefits for her children. She was surprised to learn
that the unemployment benefits would end if she went to college,
but the public assistance would continue for her children, at least
for a while. She learned from the outplacement service the plant
provided before it closed down that she could better support her
children if she went to the local community college to take
courses in graphics and publications design. These courses
would build on the skills she had acquired in the printing plant
and make her more employable in today's printing industry. She
could combine financial aid from the community college for herself with public assistance for the children.

Here is the college's calculation of her costs and financial aid
package and her own calculation:

Expenses	College's Figures	Amy's Figures
Tuition/Fees	$ 400	$ 400
Books	600	600
Room/Board/Personal	6,200	9,400
Child Care		2,600
Total	$7,200	$13,000
Minus Student Contribution	0	0
Equals Need	$7,200	$13,000

Financial Aid	Offered	Received/Accepted
Grants	$2,300	$ 2,300
Loans	2,625	2,625
Work	2,275	4,075
Other		
(Public Assistance)		$ 4,000
Total Financial Aid	**$7,200**	**$13,000**

As with Cecile, the student contribution is zero because income is less than $12,000; and the college's estimate of expenses is far lower than the student's. Amy could have appealed for child-care costs, but that was simply one more administrative hurdle to leap, and she couldn't make the effort. However, she knew that she would continue to receive the public assistance benefits, and those benefits, along with the grant, loan and on-campus employment offered, would be enough to support study for an academic year.

It's good public policy to provide public assistance for the support of children while the parent is going to college. After all, the parent is engaging in behavior that will increase his or her earning ability. Therefore, in some jurisdictions students, or their children, can qualify for public assistance. Public assistance agencies have their own rules about who can qualify for benefits. Some will provide public assistance for the student and the student's dependents under some conditions; some will provide only food stamps, medical benefits or other support. Rules vary from state to state and even from county to county within a state.

Many public assistance agencies will provide no assistance if you are employed. If you get a job, you or your children lose public assistance. However, if the employment is a particular kind of financial aid—a Federal College Work Study job—which is offered on a need basis, then the student may be able to keep the public assistance and the student employment. The best advice for parents who are considering postsecondary education is to check out the public assistance eligibility rules in the locations near the colleges and universities which they are considering.

RICH BLACK'S RULE #26.
Public assistance can provide support, particularly for the parent student's dependents. Check it out: you may be able to attend college and increase your employability if you or your children are supported.

4

John

An unemployed father of two with veteran's
benefits who also illustrates a detailed
calculation of student contribution and appeal
of that calculation. He attends a state university.

John is a veteran and a 26-year-old divorcee with two children. He can count on $555 a month in veteran's benefits. He left the Army in February of the previous year and earned $24,000 working in construction for his brother. He has $5,000 left from some assets he held with his ex, who left him to join an artist's commune in Arizona.

John illustrates several new concepts for our discussion. First, like hundreds of thousands of American men and women, he will be using Montgomery GI Bill benefits to pay for a part of his education. He also lets us examine the calculation of a student's contribution from "base year" income in detail and the possibility of appealing that calculation.

Like Cecile and Amy, John set out his expenses and completed the FAFSA. He also contacted the Veteran's Administration, which told him that when he was admitted to a college or university he could begin the paperwork for his monthly stipend. (You will find some more detail on veteran's benefits on page 89 in

Part C.) John had served for two years and qualified for $20,000 worth of educational benefits. The VA told him he would qualify for $555 each month paid over 36 months. He was surprised that he still needed and qualified for financial aid in addition to his veteran's benefits, but his VA benefits were a major support for college, so let's note them with a rule.

RICH BLACK'S RULE #27.
VA benefits are a solid foundation to which other financial aid programs can be added to pay for a college education.

Unlike Cecile, John's base year income is more than $12,000—it was $24,000—so he will have to make a student contribution of $504. While $504 is a modest amount, he wanted to understand how it was derived anyway. How do we calculate student contribution and what can a student do about it? On page 51 I presented the basic formula for determining student contribution. Now I will present the full detail. This explanation of the calculation of student contribution is rather lengthy; many people will want to skip to page 85 to review John's financial aid package. In addition, Section C-7 (page 115) illustrates the appeal process for professional judgement which would be used to override the student contribution based on previous year's income.

Here is the calculation of John's student contribution:

1. Income	$24,000
2. Less Federal Taxes	2,200
3. Less Social Security Tax	1,836
4. Less State Tax (California)	1,680
5. Less Employment Expense Allowance	2,500
6. Less Income Protection Allowance	13,490
7. Available Income	$ 2,294
8. Assets	not considered
9. Less Asset Protection Allowance	not considered
10. Available Assets	not considered
11. Adjusted Available Income (line 7 plus line 10)	$ 2,294
11. Parent Student Contribution from Adjusted Available Income	$ 504

John set up an appointment with me to complain about the whole idea that because he has earned $24,000 in the last calendar year, he somehow should have to contribute $504 for the coming academic year. First, I showed him the arithmetic that led to the calculation.

"Look," he said, "why does what I made in a previous calendar year, say 1994, have anything to do with how much I can contribute for the following academic year, which would be 1995–96, when I'm not working in '95–'96?

"Because we can verify your 1994 income by looking at a copy of your tax form," I answered. "We assume that the income we can verify is the best statement of your income until you appeal and document a lesser income. Financial aid officers have to have documentation."

His face took the look he might use when giving directions to a foreign tourist looking for the Golden Gate Bridge. "I worked full-time in 1994. In 1995–96 I can't work full-time because I will be going to college. So use my '95–'96 income, not my '94 income."

"Good point." I replied. "Once you have actually stopped working, you can file an appeal based on estimated year income.

It won't increase your Pell Grant much, because your student contribution is $504, and therefore the most your Pell Grant can increase is $504 from $1,796 to $2,300. But pick up the appeal form from the financial aid office."

"So if I don't appeal, and I make it through the first year, what do you use for the next academic year?" His voice had a resigned, you-can't-fight-city-hall tone.

I tried to hold out hope and said, "For academic year 1996–97 we would use the 1995 income, and for '97–'98 we would use the 1996 income. So by your second or third year you might have income under $12,000 and have zero contribution." I could tell he wasn't excited by an opportunity 18 months away.

He had written $504 on the pad in his lap. "So, do I have to pay the $504 before you will give me any money?"

"No," I answered. "We figure the $504 before we calculate how much you will receive. You don't have to pay it before you get your financial aid. When you have to pay it depends on lots of things. That might be the money you use for some of your books or the campus parking permit. Let's keep going."

"Damn, your logic is screwy." He was shaking his head.

I tried my polished expert spiel: "We lend and grant billions of dollars to millions of students, and if we couldn't figure in data based on students' income tax forms, we would be asked to grant and lend billions more. Right now, the government can't appropriate billions more."

Truth be told, John made some excellent points. But on the other hand, there really isn't enough grant money to help all the independent students get everything they need for a college education. Therefore the eligibility rules for independent students are to some extent rationing devices. But independent students do get some grant money, and they also receive more loan funds than there were in the '80s. So perhaps the best approach is to fill out the forms, see what you get, and then appeal if you need more. One way or another there is enough financial aid to support your undergraduate education.

RICH BLACK'S RULE #28.
Your student contribution is the amount you are expected to provide, probably from a student job, if you and a spouse made more than $12,000 in the prior calendar year. When you cease working, you can appeal.

As I noted before the long digression on student contribution, John completed the FAFSA and chose to attend the major public university in his home state of California, where the tuition, which is called "fees" in that state, comes to $4,400. He put together a budget of $18,800 as listed below, and then entered in the financial aid he would receive from various sources.

John must use ingenuity to provide for living expenses for himself and his daughters. He had earned $24,000 in the previous year, which was $18,000 after taxes, and he spent all of that to support his two daughters and himself. However, he knew that he would need to reduce his expenses further, so he set up a budget

Expenses	Amount
Tuition/Fees	$ 4,400
Books	600
Room/Board/Personal	10,200
Child Care	3,600
Total	$18,800
Minus Student Contribution	504
Equals Need	$18,296

Financial Aid	Offered/Accepted
Grants	$ 5,400
Loans	4,500
Work	1,796
Other (VA Benefits)	6,660
Total Financial Aid	**$18,356**

for room, board and personal expenses of $850 a month. Since rent was $600, he had a real problem until he found a landlord who was willing to let him live for a reduced rent in exchange for maintenance tasks in his apartment complex. Now he gets awakened at 3 A.M. to fix an overflowing toilet, but rent is reduced to $300 a month for himself and his daughters, and that's pretty good for a two-bedroom apartment in California.

John got grant assistance equal to full fees (tuition) through a scholarship program offered by his state, the Cal Grant Program, because he read the instructions carefully, completed the FAFSA by the March 2 deadline, and made sure that his high school submitted a grade transcript to the California Student Aid Commission in a timely manner.

Then there is John's loan for $4,500. John doesn't like the idea of a loan at all, and when he told his father about it the old man whistled and said, "Son, you are crazy. You are going to borrow money you can't pay back, and those finance boys will make an ass of you. You won't buy a car on credit, furniture, nothing."

But John had considered the issue carefully: by reading information that came with the student loan application, he figured that his payments would be $13 per thousand per month. If he borrowed $4,500 a year and he did that for four years, he would borrow a total of $18,000. So 18 times $13 would be $234 a month in payments. With a college degree he could get a job that would pay at least $234 a month more than the job he would get without the degree, and the job with the college degree would have a greater likelihood for promotion. He even looked at the downside. If he could not get a job using his degree as soon as he graduated, he would have to go back to construction for a while. In that case he figured he still could make his payments, he would not have to default and sooner or later that college degree would get him a better job.

In the case of Cecile, a loan for the freshman year was a poor idea because she was earning so little before she went to college. In the case of Amy, a minimal loan was there from the beginning. At least she was a mature person and could calculate the benefits.

For John, who has the ability to get a construction job, and who carefully considered the expenses and the benefits of a loan, the loan is a good investment. So while I have several rules against borrowing elsewhere in this book, in this case I will state the positive aspect of borrowing for education.

RICH BLACK'S RULE #29.
Loans can be a good investment for parent students. Figure the loan repayments. If they are less than the additional amount you can make with the college degree, go ahead and take the loan.

5

Tricia

A full-time worker using employee benefits to study part-time at a state university

Tricia is another one of our single moms, with a four-year-old son and a minimum-wage job. She works in the mail room of a catalogue sales company where most of her work is collecting the packages that have been ordered through a toll-free number and stacking them for the UPS drivers. Tricia has been with the company for three years. In that time the company has already computerized several processes. While no one has been laid off, some people who have left have not been replaced, and yet they are shipping more boxes now than they were just two years ago. Her future, thinks Tricia, is not in shipping boxes.

Her company is owned by a megacompany from Minneapolis, and that company, like thousands of large and even small employers, is really big on education benefits. At Tricia's company, once you have been on the payroll for a year the employer will reimburse you for any class that leads to a degree as long as you get at least a C in the class. Plus the employer will pay for required books.

RICH BLACK'S RULE #30.
Employer education benefits are a great way to pay for undergraduate degrees. Find out what your employer's rules are and take advantage of them.

Tricia asked the personnel manager what kind of a degree she should get, and he directed her to a career counseling center at the local state university. They had her fill out an interest inventory questionnaire and matched her interests with those of different groups. People with her characteristics seemed to be able to take on any task, so Tricia started taking courses in two areas that interested her: English and commercial art. She was preparing herself to work in advertising at some point in the future.

The local state university charges $1,000 a quarter. She had to shell out the tuition money for the first quarter, but the company paid her back when it was over. Now she takes two courses every quarter, turns in her grades and her billing statement showing she paid, and Minneapolis Megacompany sends her a check. She uses that to buy books and pay fees for the next semester.

There's another deal: since she's a parent, she qualifies for a Pell Grant because she earns less than $12,000 a year. So she gets a $1,150 Pell Grant. She would get a $2,300 grant if she could study full-time, but of course she can't, because she works full-time. She figures $1,150 is better than a poke in the eye with a sharp stick, and uses it to keep her old car running from home . . . to the babysitter's . . . to work . . . to the state university . . . to the babysitter's . . . and back to home again. True, at this rate it will take her eight years to finish her bachelor's degree. But by the time she is 30, and her boy is 12, she'll be prepared for a career with an advertising agency writing copy or designing layouts or something like that. She hopes that there are little boxes to be delivered to the UPS man for the next eight years, but even if there aren't, she is sure to be in a better position than if she didn't go to class.

Here are the college's and Tricia's calculations of financial aid. If this illustration applies to you, go over the example line by line. Tricia's employer educational benefits allow her to study while taking out minimal loans. By the way, employer benefits could be used for graduate study as well. See Section D-3, which begins on page 136.

Expenses	College's Figures	Tricia's Figures
Tuition/Fees	$ 3,000	$ 3,000
Books	600	600
Room/Board/Personal	6,200	6,800
Child Care	3,600*	3,600
Total	$13,400	$14,000
Minus Student Contribution	0	0
Equals Need	$13,400	$14,000

* Granted by financial aid office after appeal.

Financial Aid	Offered	Received/Accepted
Grants	$ 1,150	$ 1,150
Loans	2,625	900
Work	9,625	8,950
Other (Employee Benefits)		3,000
Total Financial Aid	**$13,400**	**$14,000**

6

Simmons and June

Two parent students with two financial aid packages at a major state university

What happens when two parent students are married? Each gets a financial aid package, and the results can be quite supportive. Simmons and June are married and have a two-year-old child. Both are juniors at a major state university. Each applies for financial aid by filling out a separate FAFSA, but the combination of their financial aid awards allows both of them to attend college full-time. Both of them work part-time, but because there are two of them, they arrange their schedules so often one of them can take care of the baby. They do have some child-care expenses. Simmons documented them, appealed, and had them added to his cost of education. The table below demonstrates the serendipitous fiscal synergy between these two scholars, which shows that while two can't live as cheaply as one, a couple can pool their resources and support both children and education.

Study the tables on the next page. Previous tables in this section have frequently shown that financial aid officers calculate lower costs for parent students and then demonstrated how parent students have compensated for the higher costs they face through additional work or other resources such as employee benefits or outside scholarships. This table is different. It simply shows the financial aid packages as calculated for both parent students, and demonstrates that when these are added together, there can be sufficient money for sustenance and study.

Expenses	Simmons's Figures	June's Figures
Tuition/Fees	$ 3,000	$ 3,000
Books	600	600
Room/Board/Personal	8,000	8,000
Child Care	2,600*	
Total	$14,200	$11,600
Minus Student Contribution	0	0
Equals Need	$14,200	$11,600

* Included after appeal to financial aid office.

Financial Aid	Offered/Accepted	Offered/Accepted
Grants	$ 3,000	$ 3,000
Loans	5,200	3,600
Work	6,000	5,000
Total Financial Aid	**$14,200**	**$11,600**

Note several things about this budget. First, there are two financial aid awards: both students are aid applicants, both qualify for the $2,300 Pell Grant and some additional grants from the institution. Assuming both are in their last two years of undergraduate study, each will qualify for up to $5,500 of loan assistance, although June borrows only $3,600. Each can earn $6,000—$3,000 during the academic year and $3,000 during the summer. Again, June does not need to earn this much and therefore earns only $5,000.

RICH BLACK'S RULE #31.
Two students who are married have two financial aid packages. It's possible for a married couple to finance a postsecondary education.

7

Sylvia

A forty-something mom completing an engineering degree at a private university. She illustrates the benefits of two family members in college.

Sylvia is 44 years old. She has a husband, a daughter who is a high-school freshman and a son who is a high-school senior. In the previous year she and her husband filed a 1040 listing $44,000 of taxable income from his job as a high-school English teacher. She completed an Associate of Arts degree at a community college some years ago, and now wants to complete her bachelor's degree with a goal of becoming a civil engineer. The assets that she and her husband share, not counting their home equity, are $23,000. Sylvia has no additional child-care expense, since her children are old enough to take care of themselves.

Sylvia figures her expenses differently from Cecile, Amy, John and Tricia. To her way of thinking, tuition, fees and books are her only educational expenses; room, board, and incidental expenses are already part of the family budget. The parent students discussed earlier have chosen public institutions to keep costs as low as possible. Sylvia chose a private institution because it has a reputable civil engineering department with what she found to be a truly student-centered faculty. When she visited the admissions office, a faculty member met her, asked her into her laboratory and explained research on utility pole decay she was doing with undergraduate students.

Like the other students, she filed a FAFSA, a Free Application for Federal Student Aid, before the college's deadline, which was the earliest any of our students have encountered, February 15. She calculated her expenses as shown below. The college also calculated her expenses and her student contribution and offered her a financial aid package. The two sets of calculations are quite different. Study the tables below and you will see that the college attributed room and board expenses to Sylvia that she did not perceive that she had and then expected a student contribution which she did not feel she could make. In the end she simply borrowed and worked to get the money to pay for her degree.

Expenses	College's Figures	Sylvia's Figures
Tuition/Fees	$12,000	$12,000
Books	600	600
Room/Board/Personal	7,800	0
Child Care	0	0
Total	**$20,400**	**$12,600**
Minus Student Contribution	3,918	0
Equals Need	**$16,482**	**$12,600**

Financial Aid	Offered	Received/Accepted
Grants	$ 0	$ 0
Loans	10,500	7,600
Work	5,982	5,000
Other	0	0
Total Financial Aid	**$16,482**	**$12,600**

RICH BLACK'S RULE #32.
If you're a parent student with a spouse who can support you and your children, then your out-of-pocket expenses for college will be much lower than your calculated financial aid budget. You may be able to overlook the student contribution, and easily earn and borrow enough for your college education.

While she agreed that she could borrow the money to pay her tuition, she asked me, "How in the name of cats with green paws could I be required to make a student contribution of $3,918? And why do they tell me to borrow more money than I need?"

She wanted to know the answer to these questions, so I walked her through it. If you want to know, follow along. If you don't, skip to the bottom of these tables. This is a repeat of the exercise I went through for John starting on page 65, and to find all the supporting tables you will need the "Counselor's Handbook for Postsecondary Schools" I mentioned on page 8.

1. Income–Sylvia and her husband	$44,000
2. Less Federal Taxes	4,300
3. Less Social Security Tax	3,366
4. Less State Tax (California)	3,700
5. Less Income Protection Allowance	16,670
6. Available Income	$15,964
7. Assets	$23,000
8. Less Asset Protection Allowance	35,400
9. Available Assets	0
10. Adjusted Available Income (line 6 plus line 9)	$15,964
11. Contribution from Adjusted Available Income*	$ 3,918

* Actual marginal contribution rates listed in "Counselor's Handbook for Postsecondary Schools."

But then I asked to see her offer letter, and I showed her that she and her school had entirely different assumptions about her expenses. Their budget, in the "College's Figures" column above, assigned her the same living expenses as they would have were she an 18-year-old living on her own, while she assumed that her living expenses would continue to be covered by her husband's salary. Therefore the college subtracted the student contribution (which she would find most difficult to exact from the family budget each year) from the higher budget (which was more than her out-of-pocket expenses each year) to come out with a need of $16,482. In contrast, she figured that her budget was simply the out-of-pocket expenses for tuition, and that she had no student contribution. Both positions make perfect sense if you understand the different rationales. Her own need figure was several thousand dollars lower at $12,600. She was willing to work 10 hours a week during the academic year and work full-time during the summer to earn $5,000 to pay the bills.

Sylvia figured that she would borrow $15,200 ($7,600 per year for two years) in order to complete her engineering degree, and she would begin as a civil engineer with an annual salary of at least $30,000, or a monthly salary of $2,500. Her monthly payments would be 15.2 times $13, or $198. Her take-home pay should be at least $1,875 a month, from which she would have to subtract the $198 loan payment. Not only would she have the fulfillment of a professional degree, she would also have $1,677 a month more to supplement her husband's paycheck. Finally she would be able to renovate the kitchen and buy new carpets for the house.

When I saw Sylvia recently, I mentioned that actually her student contribution for herself and her parent contribution for her son would go down a lot in the following year because she would have two family members in college, herself and her high-school senior who would then be a college freshman. That might make her needy enough to get her some grant money from her own college, but it would certainly make her son more needy and therefore he would certainly get more aid, and possibly get more grant. I said in Part A at the end of the parent contribution section (pages 7–13) that parent contribution was divided by the number of family members in college, and I dedicated Rule #6 to explain it. In the case of the parent student, the student contribution is divided by the number of family members in college, and this again has the effect of increasing financial aid.

RICH BLACK'S RULE #33.
Family contribution is divided by the number of family members who are at least half-time students for at least one term. It's economical to have parents and children in college at the same time.

To see the full impact of what I am saying, look back to the example of Daisy on page 18. You can see that her parents' income is $40,000, which is not so different from Sylvia's husband's income of $44,000. If Daisy's mother were to go back to college so there would be two students in the family, the parent contribution would be cut in half from $4,000 to $2,000. Daisy's need at Ohio State would then be $8,175 instead of $6,175, and she might receive some of that additional assistance in grant aid.

The Timeline and the Checklist
The timeline is different for parent students. After all, the first question that must be answered is, "What about the children?" If you don't have your high-school diploma, you have to get a GED, a certificate of General Educational Development. That can take time. Arranging child care can take time. Deciding what you want to study can take time, but since the degree itself will quite likely take more time, it's important that the student make a good choice of major the first time. It's harder for me to put dates on the timeline than it was for dependent students in Part A. I don't want to hassle you! I don't want you to feel guilty for missing a deadline. I just want you to do it: get that degree. Therefore, do it as soon as you can.

You do need to know that the deadlines are set by people

thinking primarily about single students, and you will get the best financial aid packages if you meet those deadlines. But I know you have the kids and probably your work on your mind as well. So I left the dates blank. Do it as soon as you can. Maybe you won't get the best package of aid the first year. The deadlines for institutional and state aid can be months before the term begins. But Pell Grants, Stafford Loans and some other aid programs will accept applications well into the academic year. And by the second year, you will know the deadlines and rules, and things will get better. Just do it!

The Timeline and the Checklist

What	When	Done?
Fill out the FAFSA to get an idea of your student contribution.	When you decide that college is right for you	
Take a look at colleges in your area. What are their costs? What do they teach? Is it worth moving your family to another area to attend college?	Do it now	
List college admissions application deadlines and meet them.	Right away	
After January 1—but before college deadline— fill out FAFSA and college financial aid forms.	First of the year	
Read financial aid offer letters from colleges that admit student. How much grant and scholarship? How much loan and work?	Spring of the year, or when they send them to you	
Fill out supplemental forms that financial aid office will provide. Make payments when they are due.	Meet the deadlines on the forms	

The Timeline and the Checklist (*continued*)

What	When	Done?
Check on public assistance benefits in areas near the college you may attend.	On a long lunch hour	
Check on educational benefits offered by your employer.	Any slow day at work	
If you qualify for veteran's benefits, review their forms and dates for submission.	Another long lunch hour	
Keep copies of all forms. Note deadlines for next year's applications.	Always	
Check out application procedures for any local scholarships including church, service clubs, fraternal lodges, ethnic organizations and athletic scholarships.	Best to start in the fall	
Discuss plans with your spouse. Check with your children's other parent, your family, relatives and friends. Will any of them help, if not with cash then maybe babysitting?	Saturday mornings over coffee	
Miss the deadline? Apply late and appeal. Some programs take applications well into the school term.	After the deadlines	

Part C
Special Categories of Students

Check below to see if you or your child fits a category

Part C of *The Complete Family Guide to College Financial Aid* focuses on six unique kinds of financial support and then gives advice on appealing for professional judgement that everyone can use. So most people will scan the first six categories: probably no more than 20% of a graduating high school class has the interests, aptitudes or qualifications for one of these scholarships. But for those who do, the benefits can be significant. More people should read the last section on appealing for professional judgement, because many families have unique circumstances.

1

Christopher

A candidate for the service academies

Is your son or daughter interested in a military career? For most parents, unless there is a strong military tradition in the family, this is a rather puzzling question. I mean, how do you know if a 17-year-old is going to be the next General Schwarzkopf; the next Chairman of the Joint Chiefs of Staff, Colin Powell; let alone the next General Hickerson? (General Patricia Hickerson is the Adjutant General of the Army and one of the highest-ranking women in the armed services of the United States.)

And why are we talking about the service academies in this chapter? Because they provide an education at almost no cost to the student or the parent. The services provide the education in exchange for a minimum of five years of service after graduation. Now, four years of rigorous undergraduate educational and military training and five years of service is not every 17-year-old's cup of tea. And if you start your junior year and don't finish, you may have a service obligation as an enlisted person. So don't encourage a student to start if he or she isn't interested.

"Well, maybe he is and maybe he isn't. How do you tell?" Christopher's mother wondered. There was no military tradition on either side of Chris's family. But Chris seemed to be a natural leader. His mother sent off for the recruiting material from the military academies and learned that of 1,340 candidates admitted in a recent year to West Point, The United States Military Academy, 1,190 were varsity athletic letter winners, 900 of them were in National Honor Society, and 513 were in scouting. Over 85%

were in the top 20% of their class. Christopher fit the profile: maybe he was cut out for a military career.

She did the next logical thing. She asked Chris what he thought about West Point.

"Hey, Mom, sounds cool. Can't you see me playing for Army against Navy? Let's apply and see what they say."

His mother still had her doubts. Would he like the discipline and the routine? His room was a such a mess she couldn't see the floor some days, and he never followed her instructions. Why would he take orders from an upperclassman? So she called me and I put Christopher in touch with a West Point graduate who explained the "whole person" concept to Chris. The military academies recruit young men and women who have (1) outstanding academic records, (2) leadership potential as demonstrated in offices held in extracurricular activities; and (3) are physically, medically and mentally qualified. Chris met those criteria. He decided he would continue to explore the academies because, while he was not certain that he wanted a lifelong military career, he could use a military career as preparation for a political position or a high corporate job. American history was full of such men.

Now, which academy? There are three, or four, or five, depending on how you count. In alphabetical order they are:

United States Air Force Academy
Director of Admissions
U.S. Air Force Academy CO
80840

United States Military Academy
Director of Admissions
606 Thayer Road
West Point NY 10996-9901

United States Coast Guard
  Academy
Director of Admissions
15 Mohegan Avenue
New London CT 06320-4195

United States Naval Academy
Candidate Guidance Office
United States Naval Academy
Annapolis MD 21402-5018

United States Merchant Marine
  Academy
Director of Admissions
Kings Point NY 11024-1699

The application process for most colleges and universities begins in the fall of the student's senior year. For the military academies, it's best to begin during the spring of the junior year, because there are so many more steps than for a conventional college or university. West Point, Annapolis, Kings Point and The Air Force Academy require that you obtain a nomination from the President, the Vice President or a member of Congress. In addition, you must qualify academically; you must pass a medical examination; you must pass a physical aptitude examination; and then you must be selected by the academy. The Coast Guard does not require a congressional nomination, but still encourages students to begin the process in their junior year.

I have included the Coast Guard and the Merchant Marine Academy in this discussion of the military academies because financially they offer similar benefits, although the Coast Guard is not a military service as the Army, Navy, and Air Force are. Those who enter the Merchant Marine have an even more distinct career focus: to be an officer on an American commercial ship. These different career objectives are critical to students as they make their choices.

In summary, the service academies offer one of the best financial aid opportunities in the country, but they are only appropriate for a student who is dedicated to a career, which need not be lifelong, in the military. In addition, the student must have an outstanding high-school record. Third, with the exception of the Coast Guard, the student must be nominated by the President, the Vice President, a Senator or a Congressman and be accepted by the academy. This last hurdle looks most daunting, but in fact it is no worse than getting into any other highly selective college.

Most Senators and Congressmen do not pick the sons or daughters of heavy contributors to their campaigns, simply because they have lots of contributors, and they have a limited number of nominations they can make each year. No, most Congressmen nominate the students who have high scores on the SAT's and outstanding high-school records. So if your child is absolutely unknown to one of these officials, don't let that deter him or her from applying to one of the academies. The first and second hurdles are the big ones. Does he or she want a military career? Does he or she have a record of excellence? If your son or daughter meets these two tests with at least a qualified yes, encourage him or her to start the process by writing to the academies.

RICH BLACK'S RULE #34.
If your child has academic achievement and leadership potential and is physically, mentally and medically qualified, encourage him or her to consider the service academies because they are a fully subsidized educational opportunity.

The Timeline and the Checklist

What	When	Done?
Begin taking courses to prepare for a highly selective college.	Freshman year of high school	
Engage in athletics and demonstrate leadership in extracurricular activities.	Freshman year of high school	
Write appropriate academies to get detailed application instructions.	Junior year of high school	
Follow application instructions including completing forms, taking the SAT's or ACT's, applying for congressional nomination, qualifying medical exam, and physical aptitude examination.	Senior year of high school	

2

Andrew

Considering ROTC and other military options

College financing for Andrew was going to be a problem. He was the second from the oldest in a large family. His parents made a good income, but by the time they paid for the younger children at the parish schools, and the medical bills for a child that had a health condition, there didn't seem to be a lot left over for college. Andrew looked at the "Be all you can be—join the Army" ads during the early season TV football games and figured he would learn everything he could about military scholarships and benefits. Andrew wasn't gung ho military, but he was proud of his country, and if serving in the military was a way to pay for college, he would at least see what he could learn.

Andrew found so many military options his head was spinning one Saturday morning as he went through the brochures he brought home from the guidance library: Army, Navy, Air Force, Marine Corps, ROTC, Reserve, National Guard, Montgomery Bill benefits, and in-service education. His uncle, who had been in the Air Force in Vietnam and had returned to teach high-school social studies, came over that afternoon to help Andrew and his father replace the rear wheel bearings on the Colt. When his father had to run over to the parts store for a bolt, Andrew got out the brochures and asked his uncle what he thought.

The two men started writing down the options and the benefits on some newsprint left over from a church planning day. By the time his dad had come back with the bolt, they had identified these options:

OPTION 1: ROTC (RESERVE OFFICER TRAINING CORPS)

The Army, Navy and Air Force have ROTC programs that recruit and train college students to be military officers upon graduation at over 300 American colleges and universities. Sixty-five percent of Army officers, and 65% of the generals in the Army come from the ROTC programs. These programs serve students not only on the host campus, but from other colleges and universities in the same geographical area. All service branches offer scholarships of various durations to some of the students in the units. Scholarships can be for as much as full tuition and fees, a book allowance and a $1,500 a year stipend. All scholarship recipients have a service obligation after they graduate either in active duty service, reserve force duty, or a combination of both.

OPTION 2

Join the army upon graduation from high school as an enlisted person. You then have the opportunity to enroll in the Montgomery GI Bill program, which means a $100 a month deduction from your pay for the first year. At the end of a two-year service commitment you will have contributed $1,200 but the benefits paid to you when you go to college will be $11,700. If you enlist for three or four years the benefits are $14,400.

OPTION 3

Same as Option 2, but the service may have a supplemental benefit of up to $30,000 if you qualify for certain military occupational specialties, such as nuclear engineering. A person in his early 20's could begin college with up to $44,000 in benefits, which would pay for a college education outright at some state universities, and would cover a major share of the costs at other universities.

OPTION 4

The reserve programs of the four military services also offer educational benefits for students interested in reserve service concurrent with or following college. The National Guard has similar programs.

Andrew sent postcards to several of the services for further information, and completed the application for an Air Force ROTC scholarship. He didn't get it, but enrolled in the ROTC courses and other activities at his university anyway. He did get a two-year scholarship as a junior, and went to law school on an Air Force scholarship. After getting his law degree, he served as a legal officer, a public relations officer, and in several other capacities before he left the Air Force. He also qualified for a military program that repaid some of the loans he took out as a freshman and a sophomore. When last I heard of him he was on the counsel's staff of a local utility and becoming involved in county politics.

RICH BLACK'S RULE #35.
The military services offer a series of financial aid opportunities for higher education. If military life appeals to you, check out the opportunities the military services offer.

The Timeline and the Checklist

What	When	Done?
Investigate loan repayment options, Montgomery GI Bill options, college courses available while in the service, and other educational benefits available while in the service, plus National Guard benefits available when you leave the service.	Junior year of high school	
Do you wish to compete for a ROTC scholarship and go directly to college? If so, apply for admission to college and apply for a military scholarship.	Senior year of high school	
Do you wish to enlist in a service and participate in Montgomery GI Bill Benefits Program? See local recruiter.	Senior year of high school	
Investigate ROTC scholarship opportunities, reserve opportunities. See ROTC unit on local campus or reserve unit recruiter.	In college	

3

Laverne

A commitment to national service

Laverne volunteered to help teach the kindergarten kids in church when she was in the fourth grade. When she was a freshman she started a recycling program at her high school, and when she was a junior she was not only a candy striper at the local hospital, but she also volunteered to campaign for a local candidate who was running on the Green Party ticket. Although the Green Party garnered less than 2% of the vote in her state, in the precinct she organized, it got 8% of the vote, in part because Laverne got on the phone on election day and made sure every likely voter in her precinct had been reminded to vote by the time the polls closed.

As a sophomore in college she had already talked to the Peace Corps recruiter and knew what her church's overseas and domestic missionary programs required. She had also reviewed the listings at the work study section of her college's financial aid office because 5% of Federal College Work Study program employment must now be community service. But while she found these programs significant, she was really excited by AmeriCorps, the new national service program. Although she went to college in the midwest, one of her friends faxed her an application for "Summer of Service" in the summer of 1993. After initial training at Treasure Island in San Francisco, she worked on a neighborhood pride project that used local teen-agers to paint over graffiti, clean up local parks and then run a "midnight courts" project that kept a local gym open until 1 A.M. so that teen-agers had a safe alternative to the streets.

When she returned to her campus in the fall she contacted the governor's office to learn what her state would be doing about the national service program. In the spring of 1994 she learned that indeed there were two different kinds of programs through which she could perform volunteer service authorized by the National And Community Service Trust Act of 1993. One of them, Ameri-Corps, provided national service education awards of $4,725 plus minimum wage for full-time service over nine months. These funds could be used to pay for past, present or future (up to seven years) educational expenses, including tuition, books and/or vocational training. In other words, a student could use them to pay off loans, or could perform service between high school and college and then use the credits to pay for college in some later year.

Laverne found that there was a another award that fit her needs better. She could get an award for $2,363 for volunteering for 900 hours over two years if she was enrolled in college during part or all of the term. While she was finishing her own bachelor's degree, she got the part-time appointment working at a nursery that served teen-age mothers who were going to high school. Then she had some funds for her first year of work toward a master's degree in social work at the local state university. The education voucher and the minimum wage were helpful as she did what she wanted to do most: help others less fortunate than herself. She also developed skills and explored career options that were useful again and again as she completed her undergraduate degree and began her professional degree.

RICH BLACK'S RULE #36.
The Americorps program has ancillary benefits that finance education. That program and public service programs sponsored by nongovernmental agencies provide magnificent opportunities for service and self-discovery.

The Timeline and the Checklist

What	When	Done?
Check community service and off-campus, nonprofit agency listings in the financial aid office.	If awarded aid under the Federal College Work Study program	
Determine AmeriCorps programs in your location. Write or call: The Corporation for National and Community Service 1100 Vermont Avenue, N.W. Washington DC 20525 (202) 606-5000; or Call the governor's office in your state; or contact your local university community service program.	Before, during or after college	
Contact volunteer service center or program on your college campus for other volunteer opportunities. Contact volunteer opportunities through your local church or temple.	When you are exploring service opportunities	

4

Rod

Athletic scholarships

Rod's father can still hear the words on the car radio. He had made it to the airport parking lot one Friday evening in early March. He had really meant to be home in time for the game, but the connecting flight had been late out of O'Hare and he knew there was no way he would make it to the gym even for the last few minutes. He had fumbled at the radio with icy fingers before he started the car. There was the announcer: "He steals the inbounds pass, he's driving to the basket, and a perfect finger roll drops in for the score. Rod Cook puts Lakewood up with 4.9 seconds on the clock. . . . Here's the inbounds to Washington, Cook's guarding him, two . . . one . . . a desperation shot off the rim, and Lakewood wins! Lakewood wins! Lakewood wins! Cook has brought his team back from 13 down with seven minutes to go to win in regulation."

That was Rod's sophomore year; that was when his father knew beyond a doubt that his son could get an athletic scholarship at a Division I school; that was when he began to do some serious research. First, he learned from the papers and from halftime TV spots that most colleges and universities belong to the NCAA (National Collegiate Athletic Association) and that the NCAA has three divisions of member schools. Division I schools have the big-time programs: they offer scholarships in at least seven sports for both men and women. A full scholarship covers tuition and required fees, books and a stipend for most living expenses. A full scholarship does not cover all of the student's expenses, however, so she or he will have to work during the summer, or borrow several thousand dollars. NCAA rules strictly limit the amount of total financial aid a student can receive on an athletic scholarship, although they do permit the student who is eligible for a Pell Grant to receive at least a portion of that grant in addition to the athletic scholarship. That's it. Nothing more. It's against NCAA rules to buy a scholarship athlete a sports coat, an extra dinner, anything.

Not all scholarships are full scholarships. In some sports, usually sports other than football and basketball, colleges will offer partial scholarships such as half scholarships, three-quarters scholarships or scholarships for some other amount. Athletic scholarships are based on achievement and promise, not need. Sometimes students qualify for need-based and athletic scholarships, and then both the NCAA rules and the rules for need-based aid must be followed.

RICH BLACK'S RULE #37.
A full athletic scholarship covers almost all of a student's expenses. Lesser scholarships can still cover substantial amounts. Athletes will still need parental assistance, some work or loan to meet the balance of college expenses.

The more than 300 Division I colleges and universities have professional coaching staffs of defined size, and these colleges are the powerhouses. Division II colleges also have paid coaching staffs, but offer about half the number of scholarships that Division I schools offer. Division III programs do not offer any athletic scholarships and view the sports program as part of the educational experience or a student activity.

RICH BLACK'S RULE #38.
Division I athletics are highly competitive. Division III is intercollegiate athletics for personal development and the thrill of competition. Division II is somewhere in between.

How do you know if your child is of Division I caliber? He or she was most valuable player, or all-league, or went to the state competition in the sport. Not only did he or she go, but probably did well. Remember that a Division I team has a finite number of slots and scholarships, and that students have four years of eligibility. Even the largest sport, football, can offer only 85 scholarships in total, so there may be only 25 scholarships for freshmen. The tennis team can only offer 4.5 slots to men and 8 slots to women. A major Division I college may award 300 scholarships to entering and continuing students, and some of those are not full scholarships.

Well, what about Division III? Intercollegiate competition but no athletic scholarships. Camaraderie, good exercise, healthy competition, setting and meeting "personal best" goals—these are the benefits Division III athletic departments pride themselves on providing. They do have national championships where the level of competition can become keen indeed.

One young lady at a Division III college was swimming exercise laps in the pool when the lifeguard came up to her and said, "We need you on the team."

"No, I don't swim competitively. I just swim for exercise."

"For our team, you can swim competitively. We need another 500 meter freestyler. Listen, I know you can place in our league. We've got a new coach who is rebuilding the team and we're fun. No one gets bent out of shape at your times if you'll work at practice and swim the meets." The freshman was a long way from home, homesick as hell, and the lifeguard was kind of cute. She joined the team, found it to be her group of friends on campus, and in two dual meets that season, just two, she placed third.

Division II is somewhere in the middle. Sometimes Division II athletes will go on to Olympic competition or professional sports, but generally their rewards are reflected in meeting team goals and not in national sports magazines.

So what is the recruiting process for a Division I athlete? By the end of the sophomore year in high school the student has made the varsity team and has attracted notice on the sports pages of the local paper. Early in the junior year he or she should receive a questionnaire, and for a fee can provide information to a rating service. The Division I coaches will access this information early in the junior year, and send another questionnaire. The student fills it out and returns it.

At this point the dreams of glory are going strong. One boy sees himself stepping up to bat behind Barry Bonds. One girl dreams of standing on the Olympic podium for a medal in the butterfly. There's nothing wrong with these dreams: we all need them. But as a parent, you should know that there are more neurosurgeons in the United States than there are professional athletes, and there are more women in the U.S. Congress than there are American Olympic medal winners in any two consecutive Olympics. So encourage the dream, but make those students study. (P.S. I've seen law school, medical school and business school admissions committees give a little extra consideration for undergraduate athletes. Not a lot, but a little.)

RICH BLACK'S RULE #39.
Foster their dreams, but make them hit the books.

In the junior year, the mail will come. Many Division I athletic teams have a computer with 5,000 names in it, from which they expect to recruit a very few outstanding athletes who can meet their academic criteria. And so they will begin with the mail. If you have a true blue-chip athlete, you will assume a new role: guardian. The blue-chipper will have phone calls, visits, and mail galore. Your job is to get a phone answering machine and screen all calls, and keep that student at the books. Of course she or he has to keep at the practice schedule too, but by this time in an athletic career that's not a problem.

The junior year has a new hurdle for students who plan to compete in intercollegiate athletics, the "NCAA Initial-Eligibility Clearinghouse." The NCAA has set up a central data base in Iowa City to collect information from every athlete that reveals whether he or she has graduated from high school, earned at least a 2.0 grade point average in a specified set of courses, and earned more than a minimum score on the ACT or SAT test. Make sure you register with the clearinghouse by the end of your junior year. If your high school counselor or coach does not have forms for supplying this information, call the NCAA Clearinghouse at (319) 337-1492 or write to:

NCAA Clearinghouse
2255 North Dubuque Road
P.O. Box 4044
Iowa City IA 52243-4044

Coaches review the data from the rating services, observe athletes at games and practices, and scan game films. Then they may invite the athlete to visit the campus at the college's expense. So you sit down, and you go over the colleges with the student. You, the parent, walk a fine line. Choosing a college is a commitment that a student has to make for him- or herself. But you have to guide. Once the trips have been chosen, I recommend you accompany the student on the recruiting visit. You will pay your own way.

Some college coaches are paid hundreds of thousands of dollars to win. Assistant coaches are paid to produce big plays so the teams win. Most coaches and assistant coaches believe they are teachers and role models first, that the student's education is their first priority. But here and there we find coaches who believe that winning is everything, and if some boys or girls get hurt, well, life's a jungle, isn't it? These are the coaches who will say, "Hey, it's not my fault if the kid spent too much time in practice and didn't do his academics."

NO! WRONG! These are 18-to-22-year-olds who have fulfilling lives to lead long after the adrenaline of the competition wears off; they are not expendable commodities. You have to protect your child from the unscrupulous; so you have to go along on the recruiting trip. You have to shake the coach's hand and tell him or her that you expect your son or daughter to get an education. You are going to follow Rich Black's eight steps for parents:

- Size up the coach. Ask how many students graduated from the team last year (Not used up their eligibility, **graduated**!) What did students major in? What are they doing now?
- Review the academic support services for athletes.
- Review the medical support for athletes.
- Ask how many students did not have their athletic scholarships renewed and why. (Athletic scholarships are one-year contracts, not four-year contracts.)
- Ask how many have gone on to professional sports, or Olympic-level competition.
- Ask the coach how long he or she has been there and how long he or she plans on staying. (Many athletes end up playing under coaches who did not recruit them.)
- Ask where your student will fit on the team. If she's a point guard and the team already has a sophomore point guard, will she get her minutes on that team?
- Talk to the parents of other players on the team.

When you have done all this, you have done your best. Advise your athlete where you think she or he should go, and let the process continue. Get season tickets and root for the team.

Uh-oh, the questionnaire never came. Or the inquiry never came from the right school. What happened? Well, it may be that your athlete is not good enough for Division I competition. Maybe the dream of playing-field glory is really yours as a parent, and not the student's. But you can give it one more shot. Go to a coach you trust, and ask for an honest evaluation. Is my kid scholarship caliber? Should I encourage him to go to a Division II or Division III college if he wants to compete on an intercollegiate level?

Or is it time to hang up the spikes, or the glove, or the racket, or the swim trunks, and just work out on his own or participate in intramurals? Recreational athletics and personal fitness have boomed in America in the last 20 years. Most colleges have added recreational sports facilities so everyone can play. Historians will point to that as one of the best developments in American higher education in the 20th century. It's right up there with co-education in my book.

But hey, recruiters can overlook good candidates. Sometimes a gifted athlete doesn't play for a high-profile team. Sometimes a coach isn't well known yet, so his or her players don't get the respect they deserve. So what do you as a parent do? You get that objective opinion. And then you tell the coach to call the colleges in which your son or daughter is interested. Those college coaches will return the phone call and ask for information. Want to do more? Put together a highlight video and send it. Keep it brief. But in six or seven minutes you can get the message across. That doesn't work? Then the last resort is to walk on. Most college teams have a tryout day for a place on the team. An athlete who is good enough will make the team, and an athlete who is even better will get a scholarship in the upperclass years.

Division I athletics is, as Samuel Johnson said about marriage, "the triumph of hope over experience." Let's never squelch hope in our children. As parents, let's guide them as best we can to rewarding experiences. If that means a scholarship on a Division I team, great. But sooner or later they will find a level of athletics at which they cannot compete. If that level is college, we need to help them find new and different hopes for different goals. Fortunately, there are plenty of financial aid programs other than athletic aid, so the decision not to compete does not preclude financial support for college.

The Timeline and the Checklist

What	When	Done?
Assess student's athletic excellence.	Sophomore year of high school	
Meet requirements of NCAA National Clearinghouse.	Junior year of high school	
Complete questionnaire sent by rating services and colleges in which you are interested.	Junior year of high school	
Take up to five paid recruiting visits if offered by teams in this sport. If not offered, visit coach on campus being considered. Or send a letter of inquiry with a videotape, summary of athletic achievements and an academic transcript.	Senior year of high school	
Sign a letter of intent with college that best meets your needs.	Senior year of high school	
If not on a full scholarship, apply for financial aid according to the regular schedule for your college.	Senior year of high school	

5

Stephen

A student with a disability

People are different: most of us have obstacles to overcome. Students with disabilities have a particular set of obstacles. Disabled students do qualify for most of the need-based financial aid programs I discussed above, and then there are several special programs I want to present as well.

I first became aware of these programs when working with a sophomore, Stephen, who is blind. He came to appeal for an extension of the deadline for a financial aid application so he could continue his work-study job in the accounting office. It seems he hadn't read up on the deadline until a week after it had passed. He blamed the oversight on his Seeing Eye dog, Sarah. I asked Sarah what she had to say about the matter, and she cast her liquid brown eyes on me with some objectivity. Perhaps that look said she had her head full just following Stephen's instructions; filling out forms was my problem. I noted that he was blind and we had no braille instructions in his folder, so the auditors would know why I made an exception and granted his appeal so that his application could be considered to have been filed on time. Stephen went on to law school, actually, and was working for an Air Force procurement unit in Sacramento when I last caught up with his progress.

Then I tried to find out what I could about the unique programs that provide financial support for disabled students in addition to those for which all students are eligible. I learned there are five special programs for disabled students that provide support in addition to financial aid for undergraduate and graduate students.

These programs vary from locality to locality and do not necessarily have the same rules or benefits. You as the parent, or you as the student if you do not have the support of your parents, must apply separately for each of these programs and be prepared to understand carefully what each program is designed to do. You also need to know how the student might take advantage of that purpose to pay for college. For example, is this a program designed to return a worker to gainful employment? If so, consider your son or daughter a worker and make the point that a college education is required to obtain that employment. Or is this a program to help students accommodate a specific disability? A student may be considered on the basis of parental income for one program and not for another. You need to understand the program's goals so you can advocate clearly and firmly for eligibility. You may have to pioneer for a benefit due to a disability with a particular agency or organization.

Is there a local "center for independent living" that can provide assistance and the support of a community? These centers have come into being in the last 25 years to provide community, counseling and advocacy for students with disabilities. Usually they are not residential facilities, but they are essential sources of information and other support for disabled students. Frequently a disabled student's situation is unique; occasionally the student has difficulty articulating a concern; and finally, many clerical staff in social service agencies simply don't know all the rules and exceptions to those rules that can benefit disabled students. A center for independent living and the campus disabled students office can provide additional advocacy that can get the disabled student the assistance to which she or he may be entitled.

In addition, you need to find out what support is available at the college or university you wish to attend. Are all of the classrooms accessible? Is there an office or program for disabled students? What is the university's policy for "satisfactory academic progress" for disabled students? Federal financial aid regulations require that a student maintain a given level of academic achievement, pass a certain number of courses at defined intervals and graduate before a finite time period. These regulations are made to insure that students without disabilities do not unduly prolong their education in order to receive financial aid. What standards does the school have for students with disabilities? Can exceptions be made?

Will the university make special allowances for the increased costs that a disabled student must face? For example, students with learning disabilities must frequently take a battery of examinations to fully document the nature of the disability so that the college can make an appropriate accommodation. These tests can cost several hundred dollars or more. Will the college provide financial aid to cover the costs of these tests? If not, will the college at least allow testing as a cost, so that if another organization pays for the test, the financial aid office does not reduce the other aid the student receives? These are important questions that need to be resolved before the student begins study or as soon as the disability is identified.

Is the financial aid office willing to recognize hidden disabilities? Students with learning disabilities, sickle cell anemia, or chronic fatigue syndrome are often indistinguishable from other students. Once they are identified, does the college have a way of extending accommodations? For example, can it increase grant aid for these students, or will it offer special assistance in finding appropriate employment rather than offering loans? Colleges and universities vary in their ability to be of assistance, but students with disabilities, and their parents, must at least determine that personnel and policies are as encouraging as the law requires and support allows.

Students with disabilities have special challenges when taking federal loans. There are indeed clauses in the promissory note that state that if the student becomes disabled, he or she need not repay the loan. The operant word is "becomes." If the student knew of a disability at the time that he or she signed the promissory note, then the student cannot subsequently ask that the loan be canceled because of the disability. Such a student must repay the loan, and if she or he does not, the loan will be considered in default and the student will not be eligible for any form of financial aid.

> **RICH BLACK'S RULE #40.**
> **There are special financial assistance programs for students with disabilities.**
> **Check them out on a program-by-program basis.**

Here are five programs and the benefits they provide:

1) SUPPLEMENTAL SECURITY INCOME (SSI)

Benefits   A monthly stipend for living expenses. Amounts vary from state to state, and are different for blind students. Students who receive SSI may also qualify for Medicaid insurance benefits.

Qualifications   Must be unemployable because of a disability and must not have personal resources above a given economic level.
If over 18, may be considered eligible independent of parents' resources.

Where to Apply   Local office of U.S. Social Security Administration. (See "Government" section of local phone book.)

2) SOCIAL SECURITY DISABILITY INSURANCE (SSDI)

Benefits   A monthly stipend for living expenses. Amounts vary depending on the work experience of the wage earner.
Medicare benefits, which pay 80% of hospitalization, may also be covered.

Qualifications   This is a program for disabled workers. Therefore the student must have worked a certain number of years. In some circumstances, the disabled child of a retired, disabled or deceased parent may qualify for benefits. There is no limitation on the recipient's assets.

Where to Apply   Local office of U.S. Social Security Administration.
                        (See "Government" section of local phone book).

3) MEDICAID

Benefits   Medical insurance, for full or partial coverage of hospitalization,
                        doctor visits, medicines, etc.

Qualifications   Supplemental Security Income recipients, and students who
                        qualify for other programs in some states, may qualify for Medi-
                        caid benefits.

Where to Apply   Local office of U.S. Social Security Administration.
                        (See "Government" section of local phone book.)

4) IN-HOME SUPPORTIVE SERVICES (IHSS)

                        (May go by another name in some jurisdictions)

Benefits   Attendant care or personal care for students. Some attendants live
                        with students.

Qualifications   Must be eligible for Supplemental Security Income and be recom-
                        mended by a physician. May not be available in all states.

Where to apply   County social services (welfare) office.
                        (See "County Government" section of phone book.)

5) VOCATIONAL REHABILITATION

Benefits   Payment of tuition and fees, supplies, certain equipment, and
                        other expenses.

Qualifications   Applicant must show promise of employability and self-support
                        with additional training, but be currently unable to work.

Where to Apply   State Department of Vocational Rehabilitation.
(See "State Government" section of phone book.)

The Timeline and the Checklist

What	When	Done?
Determine disability and set a long-term learning strategy.	Preschool, elementary school, as soon as possible	
Review criteria for Supplemental Security Income contribution.	Junior year of high school, or younger if parents have low income and limited resources	
Review critera for Social Security Disability Insurance.	When parent is disabled, retired or deceased	
Review criteria for In-Home Support Services.	When applying for Supplemental Security Income	
Review criteria for Department of Vocational Rehabilitation services.	While student is in high school	
Apply for all of the above programs for which you qualify.	Senior year of high school, if haven't done already	
Apply for the regular financial aid programs.	January through March of senior year	

6

Max

Applying for special scholarships

Max's mother, Clara, long ago recognized that her son had two levels of energy, high . . . and turbocharged. She let him take two paper routes in the fifth grade so he would calm down by the time he got to the breakfast table. My goodness, the boy could drive you crazy with his questions and his comments. Then he comes to the fall of his senior year in high school, and he gets hit by a BMW from Mt. Vernon: broke his pelvis in two places so the doctor puts him in a body cast and says he'll be at home for six weeks. Max in a body cast was like an alarm clock in a tin pail. He was demanding, he was shouting, he literally bounced up and down on the bed. So Sylvia got the college materials together.

"Max, I want six college applications out of you before you go back to school. And you'd better do the financial aid too."

"Mom, they won't let me do the financial aid form till January 1."

"Do it now! Here! Read this book and apply for every damn scholarship you can. You need money. They got money to give away. You get that money, and don't say another word."

Clara had gotten some college catalogues and a scholarship directory from a neighbor whose daughter had applied for colleges last year. The scholarship directory was by Daniel Cassidy, titled *The Scholarship Book*, published by Prentice Hall.

He began to systematically review the scholarship directory. Because he was so good with the computer, he entered the name and address of every scholarship in which he thought he might be interested in a file. He found it took him an hour to review 20 pages in the scholarship directory and enter the addresses of the scholarships for which he might qualify in his computer. The book was over 200 pages long, so it was a two-day, ten-hour project to identify the scholarships. Most people would have used three-by-five cards to make a list of possible scholarships, so if you are not a computer whiz, worry not; the cards will work just fine.

Then Max composed a letter asking for information and the application for each scholarship, and finally he did a "mail merge" to get the letters written. It was another hour to print out his letters. When he was done he found 20 scholarships in the Cassidy book for which he might qualify. Had he used another directory, he would probably have found the same number. If you lack Max's computer skills, you will have to type the letters by hand, but you can get it done.

Max found one scholarship for students who had been paper carriers, one for people of Hispanic heritage, one for students interested in electrical engineering, one for students from his part of the state, and one for students who had overcome an incapacitating injury. His mother wasn't sure that Max was really incapacitated, but encouraged him to apply for that scholarship anyway. The rest of the applications were more general, and some were contests, like the award sponsored by the Japanese industrialist that required an essay on world trade.

In about two weeks the applications started to arrive. By that time Max could sit up and was beginning to try his crutches, so it was much easier to assemble the forms. He read the first application and let out a loud lamentation. "Aiy . . . yae . . . yai." Every one of them wanted an essay with a topic like "Why my heritage gives me an advantage in fulfilling my obligations as an American citizen" or "The challenges engineers face in today's society" or "The importance of animals in biomedical research." Well, Max didn't shrink. He could have sent his mom to the library for research on some of those topics, but instead he used his computer to get to the information highway. He sent messages to trade associations, college professors and other experts to learn a little about each area, and then he plunged in. A 500-word essay, which most applications required, wasn't too bad. He found that he could ask questions in the first paragraph, answer them for the next seven paragraphs and wind it up in the eighth. The first essay took three hours, but by the twelfth he had it down to forty-five minutes for the first draft, and three hours for the application, references, biographical data and all.

When he was done Max had applied for 20 scholarships, which, if they all came through, would pay a total of $15,750. Well, they didn't all come through. He never heard from three of them, eight of them wrote and said they received his application but other applicants were more qualified, two wrote that they would not award the scholarship this year because their funds were limited, and four awarded him honorable mention. But then there were three actual awards: $500, $1,250 and half-tuition at the college of his choice. That last scholarship encouraged Max to accept admission and financial aid at an independent college where the tuition was $13,000. Because he had so many outside awards, Max didn't have to borrow or work his first year in college.

The second year was another story. It turned out that only the scholarship for $1,250 was renewable. So he had to use the college's self-help financial aid for his upperclass years.

RICH BLACK'S RULE #41.
Make the effort! Apply for all the special scholarships for which you are eligible. But expect that you will have to apply for the regular financial aid programs as well.

Max's mother, Clara, wondered about the computerized scholarship search services. Some were advertised on the local community college bulletin board; some were in the local newspaper. She found that the range of costs was quite amazing, from $25 to

$199. Some promised up to 20 scholarships, some only said they had a large database and would identify those scholarships for which the student qualified. So she got the parents' club at her high school interested in sponsoring students. In all, they paid the application fees for ten different services for ten students who volunteered to complete a service's questionnaire. The parents' club learned that some of the services simply sent back lists of financial aid programs that were available in government publications or the guidance office: The Pell Grant; the state grant; the Supplemental Education Grant; the Federal Family Educational Loans. And then some of the services provided as many leads as Max found by searching through the book for a scholarship for which he qualified. These services really did give lists of the unique scholarships for which each student qualified.

How could a parent or a student tell which were the better services? Well, for openers, forget about any service that charged more than $100. All of them seemed to promise much more than they delivered. And then look for those that didn't promise too much. Consider that the service is as good as the data it has, and that data probably comes from one of the directories. So maybe the student will save time by filling out a questionnaire and sending it in to a service. But the service can't guarantee anything, because there are not special scholarships to match the infinite ways that each student is unique.

Consider the odds. There are 12 million undergraduate students, but probably no more than 25,000 organizations that give scholarships, including local PTAs and Rotary Clubs with their $250 awards. And most of those organizations already have a good idea of their applicant population. So there are 50,000 or 60,000 ambitious high-school seniors applying to a couple of thousand major independent scholarship organizations. No data search service can promise a scholarship award with any integrity. Some promise to do their best to match students' characteristics with possible programs. These services are the ones that may be a good investment of $25 to $75. On the other hand, some students can do just as well perusing the books that list scholarships in the local library or high-school guidance office.

Rich Black's Rule #42.
There are rip-off search services and conscientious organizations. In general, if you want to pay a service, use the ones that advertise a large database against which the service matches the student. Beware of a search service that guarantees extravagant success.

The Timeline and the Checklist

What	When	Done?
Review directories of scholarships at libraries or high school guidance offices. Use a search service if you wish.	Spring of junior year	
Write for application in September. Make a list of application deadlines and submit forms in a timely manner.	Fall of senior year	
Wait for the acceptance letters. The more you apply, the better your chances.	Spring of senior year	

7

Olga

A student filing an appeal for "professional judgement"

When the award letter came back from the state scholarship agency, Olga's heart sank, and when the financial aid office sent its letter, she was in complete despair. Her parent contribution was over $12,000, and both the state scholarship agency and the financial aid office calculated that she had no financial need to attend the local state university. The trouble was that the parents' contribution was based on the prior year income, and that had been a very unusual year. I addressed filing an appeal in Part A-9 (see page 37) but the topic is so critical that I want to illustrate it further in this chapter as a special category.

Financial aid officers can address changes in family financial circumstances by exercising "professional judgement," a term that has a precise meaning for them and the auditors who review their work. If the financial aid officer has documentation that relates to a student's special circumstances, she or he can change one of the data elements that are a part of the calculation of the parent contribution or the student contribution. For example, if a family lost a home in a fire and had to incur additional expenses to set up a new household, the financial aid officer could reduce the family's total income, and therefore parent contribution, by some of all of those additional expenses. Such a reduction would be exercised under the concept of "professional judgement." Let's return to Olga to see what's involved in getting a financial aid award changed through professional judgement.

Olga's father was a farmer who grew mostly hay and potatoes. Last year had been the best year anyone could remember for potatoes in his part of the country. For one thing, both Maine and Idaho had bad weather, and the packing houses were looking for potatoes. Then there was a drought all up and down the north-west coast, and every dairy farmer had to buy hay. Never could anyone remember such a combination of good weather and good luck in the valley where her father farmed, except a few old-timers who said '52 had been such a year. Olga's father had paid off debt on farm machinery and paid down the mortgage on the land. There was a new Dodge Ram pickup and even a trip for the whole family to Disneyland.

But that was last year. Here it was June and the rain wouldn't stop. Potato futures were down, and the price of hay was like a dowager's hemline: low and going nowhere. Olga's father hoped he would clear expenses. He could feed his hay to his own cattle, and there would be enough from beef sales to keep food on the table and gas in the Dodge, but there wasn't any money for Disneyland this year. There wasn't even any money for college; and these letters said they wanted $12,000.

Olga wasn't going to stay on the farm without a fight. She took the letters and the Dodge and drove up to her state university. It felt funny to park near the arena where they had come for basketball games since she was a little girl and go across the campus to the basement of the administration building where they had a financial aid office. The receptionist asked to see her letter and then handed her an appeal form. Olga said, "I want to talk to a counselor. It's 60 miles from our farm. I can't come back with this form. I need to see a counselor."

The receptionist typed a message into a monitor and asked her to wait. After 30 minutes she called out, "Olga, Olga Ramirez."

"Yes."

"Mr. Connerly says he can see you about 3:30 after a staff meeting. Can you wait?"

"Yes, I'll get some lunch and come back."

Mr. Connerly was nice enough when she came in and explained her problem, but he was all business.

"Okay, now look. I can consider an appeal based on this year's income, but I need documentation. Half the farmers in the state tell me they are having a rough year, and then when I get tax forms from them the next year, guess what? Twice the income they projected. I've got auditors looking over my work, and if they think I have not exercised proper professional judgement, they can ask for the money back. Then I have to bill you, and we are both unhappy.

"I want you to go to agricultural extension or the local USDA office and get them to write a letter appraising crop returns for last year, and estimating returns for this year. I want you to bring me a statement on what you think your father's income will be this year. We may make an exception for the fall semester and then get another statement for the spring semester. Keep copies of what you submit, and expect that it will be some weeks before we consider appeals. Oh, and don't give up hope. I've had three appeals already from farm kids in that valley. My boss gives me all the farm kids. But if you can bring documentation, I can probably get that parent contribution down.

"And another thing. Get a job. Make as much as you can, because maybe you will have to replace some of the parent contribution with your own income."

Olga headed home with the appeal forms, and was at the USDA office the next day. She had her father's tax forms for the last four years to prove that last year was most unusual. She showed the "before" and "after" bills for the mortgage so the financial aid people could see where the money had gone. She even Xeroxed the truck title, but the Visa bill for Disneyland she left in the drawer. She didn't think the financial aid office wanted to make an award to cover Disneyland. And she did work every chance she got. She made the first tuition payment herself before she heard about the appeal. When it came through, indeed the letter said that the parental contribution had been reduced to about a third of what it had been. Her father still looked a little overwhelmed when she gave him the new bill, but he mumbled something like "Guess that's better than what we had, and I figured I'd have to pay something to get peace and quiet around here."

Olga kept the notes that Mr. Connerly gave her in case she had to appeal again. Here they are:

Apply for financial aid and then appeal.

Provide documentation from experts in writing.

Be exact. Don't say, "Hay went down." Say, "According to the Farmtown Co-op, hay sold for $5.00 a bale in July 1994 and is now selling for $1.75 a bale."

Keep copies of everything you submit.

Be prepared to go in person. Ask for a detailed explanation and appeal any denial, but recognize that the financial aid officer has the final say. He or she has to answer to an auditor, and knows what will pass and what won't. If your appeal is accepted, great! If it isn't, then there is little more than can be done.

RICH BLACK'S RULE #43.
In some circumstances financial aid officers can exercise "professional judgement" to increase student need, but they require clear documentation for the auditors.

Other frequently asked questions:

Can my Congressman help my appeal?
Yes, after you have tried your best with the financial aid officer. Keep letters brief and to the point. Include documentation.

Can I appeal to the college president?
Sure; follow the rules for the Congressman above, and remember that the financial aid officer will probably draft the reply for the president's signature, so be factual, brief and concise. If the college president feels the financial aid officer has been unreasonable, he will ask the vice president or dean to talk to the financial aid officer about it.

Is it better to shout or cry when making an appeal?

Save the theatrics for drama class. Financial aid counselors have work to do, and can't impress auditors with statements that they acted under the influence of fear, pity, or a stellar performance.

The Timeline and the Checklist

What	When	Done?
Assemble complete documentation on major changes in income and assets.	Before you apply for financial aid	
Secure any appeal forms used by the financial aid office at the college or university you will attend.	As soon as you know you will appeal	
Appeal and get results of appeal.	If possible, before student accepts offer of admissions	
Present appeal in person if necessary. Have questions written when you begin meeting. Be factual.		

Part D
Financial Aid for Graduate Study

1

Basic Understandings for Graduate Study

*No Parent Contribution (usually)—A Different
Vocabulary—Loans for Graduate Study*

Who should read this chapter? Well of course, parents should read it; but relax, parents—for the most part, your job is done. No parental contribution is expected because graduate students are considered independent of their parents for federal financial aid programs. Medical, law and some other professional schools collect parental income information that they use to allocate their own gift funds; a few federal financial aid programs for the health professions want parental information; but by and large financial aid officers do not expect parental contributions. If they do expect a parent contribution, they are often willing to replace it with loans. But read the chapter anyway. You can advise your children better as they are undergraduates preparing for graduate study and when they are graduate students themselves. And some parents can and do choose to provide financial support. After all, pretty soon you may be able to say, "My son, or daughter, the doctor . . . or lawyer . . . or investment banker."

RICH BLACK'S RULE #44.
For federal financial aid, graduate students are independent and no parent contribution is expected. Some professional schools ask for parental information to award grant funds.

Whether to go to graduate school? When to go and what graduate program to select? These are complex questions for any student, and more so for the parent student. First, you have to decide on the career for which you wish to prepare. No more "knowledge for its own sake"; graduate study is to prepare for a career in some area, and presumably you discerned that area through your undergraduate study, through your work experiences during and after undergraduate study, or in some other way. Next you need to know that graduate study has three broad divisions: the professions; the humanities and social sciences; and engineering and the sciences. These divisions have different financing programs, which I discuss in more detail below. Finally, admission and aid for graduate study are organized on a school or departmental basis. Though you may apply to a central admissions office, the decision on whether to admit and how much aid to offer are being made by the school and the department.

To help you evaluate which graduate program is right for you, first learn how financial aid is organized in the discipline or career area you want; next evaluate yourself as a student; and then look at the table below. Do you want the full-time program at Prestige University's law program? Or is Local University's part-time evening program more suited to your needs?

Rich Black's Graduate School Selectivity Table

Lower Selectivity	Higher Selectivity
<<<<<<<<<<<<<<<<<<<<<<<<<<<<	>>>>>>>>>>>>>
Part-time	Full-time
More Supportive	Highly Competitive
Lower Career Payoff	Higher Career Payoff

Departments at the higher end admit students with top undergraduate grades, high or outstanding scores on the Graduate Record Examination or the other tests that various disciplines require, outstanding recommendations, and a record of undergraduate achievement related to the area that you want to study.

Departments at the lower end of the selectivity scale will still require a B average in undergraduate school, although sometimes they are willing to make allowances for lower undergraduate achievement if the student has demonstrated accomplishment since graduation. These schools and departments are more likely to facilitate part-time enrollment. I'll tell you some more about these programs as we go along.

Perhaps you knew all this and what you want me to tell you is where the money is! Especially if you yourself are a parent, you want to know: "Where is the money?" And I say: "Good question!" I want you to be sure that you can answer that question before you begin graduate school. I'm going to tell you the process for finding just where all the money is found. I'll give you four illustrations of how students found the money. But I want **you** to plan it out. Some of you have an undergraduate record that will lead to one of the highly selective programs. Go for it! Some of you will find that the part-time professional programs are more affordable and more consistent with your academic preparation. Then you do that. If you have parental responsibilities, then the part-time route may be the only route available to you. I want you to get that degree, because you have a responsibility to do the best you can for your children and for yourself, and if you have been given the talents for an advanced degree, then go for it. You'll be better able to provide for yourself and your children, and you'll set the example that ambition and diligence pay off. That's what parents are supposed to do.

RICH BLACK'S RULE #45.
Survey the programs available to you. Determine your career goals, academic achievements, time and energy. Then go for that graduate degree. There's a way to finance it.

So how do you learn if there is enough of the right kind of financial aid? To answer this question, I need to tell you how graduate study is organized and the specialized vocabulary for graduate financial aid. I put graduate studies in three broad categories: (1) the professions; (2) engineering and the physical sciences; and (3) the humanities and the social sciences.

Here is the financial aid vocabulary you need:

FELLOWSHIPS

This is the good stuff, the gift aid at the graduate level. Most graduate students who get gift aid don't get grants or scholarships; they get fellowships. For university-sponsored fellowships, you apply to a department at a university and it provides the fellowship. For extramural fellowships, you apply to a foundation, government agency, or corporation for assistance. Examples of extramural fellowships are a Fulbright-Hayes award for graduate study abroad, a Ford Foundation Minority Doctoral Fellowship, or a Howard Hughes Medical Institute Doctoral Fellowship in Biological Sciences. The university will have a directory of extramural fellowships someplace on campus; look in the graduate division office, the departmental office, the career placement office, and the library. Many universities have them on microcomputer databases that allow searches on such key phrases as "cell biology" or "medieval French."

MULTIYEAR FELLOWSHIPS

These are the really good stuff. If you are the best and the brightest of applicants and you are applying to the strongest academic departments at American universities, you will be offered a fellowship for more than one year, and perhaps for your entire graduate program. All you have to do is come and perform at the level expected of you, and you will have fellowship assistance for much or all of the time it takes to complete your degree. If you can get a multiyear fellowship, get one.

GRANTS AND SCHOLARSHIPS

A few universities do use these forms of aid at the graduate level, and they have the same wonderful connotation that they have for undergraduates: they're free—aid you don't have to pay back or earn through teaching, research or some other effort.

ASSISTANTSHIPS

Aha! You have to work for these. There are teaching assistant-ships, which mean that you have to teach undergraduates, and research assistantships, which mean that you will be working on a research grant in some professor's laboratory. Generally the admissions or fellowship committee offering these awards has considered carefully the question of financing your graduate education. The assistantship plus your time in the classroom should allow you, by dint of great industry, to complete the graduate degree in a reasonable time. Assistantships have their upside and their downside. On the upside, you actually are teaching or doing research. You are gaining pivotal entry experience for the career in teaching and research to which you aspire. But on the down-side, after the first three or four years of study for the doctorate, assistantships can distract you from essential classes or your dissertation to the point that you delay in completing your de-gree, and, alas, you slip into the status of a perpetual graduate student—a status of dependency, penury and cynicism.

READERS AND TUTORS

Readers grade term papers, midterms, and finals. Your depart-ment should clearly state how many of each you will do each term and how much you will be paid. Tutors may work through the academic departments, through study centers, or even the athletic department to provide supplemental instruction. Lately, having a tutor has become fashionable; study centers have to weed out the A-minus students who want to be A-plus so they can focus on their primary clients, students who just need to catch up with the class. Some tutors have no academic affiliation; they just put up flyers on campus and work with whoever comes through the door. Since pay rates for tutors can start at $15 an hour and go up from there, this is a good way to cover some financial gaps. You should limit your efforts in this area to 15 hours a week if you can.

STIPEND

At times a graduate program will indicate that it provides a fellowship for tuition and fees, and a monthly stipend for living expenses. So the question is, does the stipend cover all the living expenses, or just part of them? That's for you to research.

Remember when I talked about undergraduate assistance I described the combination of grant, loan, and employment that constituted the financial aid package? At the graduate level the word "package" is not used as much, and there is not necessarily the assumption that the award is meeting full need. In order to assure that your aid meets your full costs, make sure you have a clear understanding of the room, board, tuition, books and incidental costs of a particular program, plus the amount you will need to support your dependents. Most universities will provide a clear statement of this information. Then make sure that the sum of all the assistance offered you meets or exceeds those costs.

LOANS FOR GRADUATE STUDY

Read this section carefully, because so much of graduate aid is provided through the loan programs. These are the same programs available at the undergraduate level: the Stafford Loans, Perkins Loans, and Direct Loans. Additional programs are the Health Education Assistance Loans for medical students and the Law Access loans for law students. The lenders are banks, the colleges themselves and sometimes organizations associated with a discipline, such as the Law Access Program. The financial aid office or the graduate admissions office can steer you toward lenders with whom it will work.

The amount borrowed can be much greater for graduates than for undergraduates because some programs, especially those in the professions, have no financial aid except loans. Some loan programs require no payments while students are in school, including undergraduate loans while the student is in graduate school, if the student files the deferment forms. Better yet, the government pays the interest on some undergraduate loans, so the interest doesn't accrue and get added to the loan principal. An exception to this rule is any loan called an "unsubsidized loan." Check with your lender about the rules for your loan program.

How much can you borrow? The Federal Family Education Loans and the new Direct Loan Program will let a graduate student borrow the entire cost of a graduate education. The statutory maximum is an absurd $138,500 for the combination of graduate and undergraduate study. But wait; the statutory limit is not the problem: tolerable debt limits are.

Let's do a little "back of the envelope" figuring and see how it applies to the cost of a graduate education and the earnings you will have to repay. Back in Part A, on page 21, I gave the rule of $13 a month per thousand. So let's try it out. Say you have been admitted to Ivy League Business School, where the cost is $30,000 a year. And it's a two-year degree, so you will have borrowed $60,000 before you sit down with the Fortune 500 recruiter. Since we just came out of a recession, your starting salary may only be $60,000, and your payments will be . . . hmm, let's see here . . . 13 times 60 . . . $780 a month! GASP! CHOKE! But let's think it through. Gross pay for $60,000 is $5,000 a month; figure take-home pay will be about $3,600 a month, and another $780 from that leaves you $2,820 to live on. Well, a lot of Americans live on $2,820 a month, and you probably can't make $60,000 without the degree, so the loan is a "good ROI," (return on investment), as you business school types might say.

We go next from "mammon," as it were, to the "sacred" and look at borrowing for a divinity school education. Unfortunately, divinity school may not cost a whole lot less than business school—the tab can easily be $25,000 a year. Say you borrow $50,000 for graduate study at Holy Divinity School. As a beginning minister you might expect to make $24,000 a year, plus a parsonage allowance. So that is $2,000 a month gross, and $1,200 a month take-home. Fifty times $13 gives you $650 a month for loan repayments, which leaves you $550 a month for granola, coffee, books and gasoline. That budget will insure adherence to the ecclesiastical tradition of poverty if nothing else does. Obviously loans are not the entire answer to financing advanced study for a degree like divinity. If you don't have help from a spouse, parents, assistance from your denomination, or some other support, you cannot undertake full-time divinity study.

As I write this chapter, four new repayment plans have just gone through the final stages of the federal regulation process: the standard repayment program, which I have discussed above; the graduated repayment plan; the alternative repayment program; and the income contingent repayment program. These repayment programs have great promise for borrowers who will enter low-income fields, but they are not yet in practice for the most part, although some features have been available for Stafford Loans for some time. I discuss them in greater detail in Appendix A.

RICH BLACK'S RULE #46.
Understand the different graduate-level vocabulary so you know how much the graduate school or department will give you, how much you have to work, and how much you have to borrow. Be sure that you can repay your loans on what you are going to earn.

Now that we have covered the vocabulary of graduate financial aid, let's review the three kinds of graduate study. We start with the professions: medicine, law, business, journalism, divinity, dentistry, architecture, public health, and education. These are master's or doctor's degree programs of two, three, or four years duration that lead to advanced employment in these professions. These are not Ph.D. programs, which are a preparation for a career in research and university teaching. We will cover those later.

2

Ramona

A candidate for a law degree
Typical of full-time students in medicine, law,
business, dentistry and other professions

Not long ago I ran into Ramona at an alumni reception. I remember the issues she faced in gaining her professional degree: career choice, parenthood, choosing the right law school, and loan repayment. Perhaps her experience will help others think about their options. First, she decided on her profession some time in junior high. She had wanted to be a lawyer ever since her policeman uncle took her brother and her to court to see a criminal trial. In high school she met a lawyer through a girls' club program sponsored by the local police department and asked if she could volunteer in her office. The lawyer offered her a contract: 15 hours of error-free filing and she had a job. Misfile a folder and you're paid for your work, but no more work; lose a file and you leave today. That lady negotiated a tough contract, but Ramona shook on the deal. She didn't misfile a document, though she did have to ask the lawyer to look in her briefcase once to discover the location of the document they were trying to find. She ended up working in that law office all the way through undergraduate school and the summer after her first year of law school. Ramona's parents made their financial contribution during college, but they made it clear they could offer no more support for graduate study, so Ramona gathered the financial aid literature for law schools.

In her senior year of college she applied to 17 different law schools of varying selectivity and reputation. She was disappointed that only two of them offered her a modest fellowship; they were both private schools that cost more than several of the lower-priced, in-state public institutions to which she was admitted, and the prestige of Major State Law School was higher. I wish professional school prestige wasn't so important, but it is. The better students and the better faculty teach at the better professional schools. Students who attend the high-prestige institutions have more and better career options.

She had another hard choice to make in her last year of college: she became pregnant and decided that law school or no, she would be a mother, and she would take a year off to get the baby started. Therefore when considering schools, she was careful to inquire about the day-care provisions on each campus.

She did find several law schools that had taken serious note of the disincentives to professional study that loans represented. Two law schools had set up loan repayment programs so that if a graduate had a hard year, or chose a less remunerative aspect of the profession (for example, public-interest law), the professional school would pay some or all of the loan payments for that year.

Next, Ramona calculated her loan payments. Three years of law school at Major State would cost her $18,000 a year, including child care. She would have to borrow all of it, or $54,000. If she took the 10-year payment plan, her payments would be $702 a month. Many graduates of Major State Law School start at $50,000 a year, or $4,166 a month. Take-home pay would be about $3,100. Subtracting the $702 monthly loan payment would still leave her $2,398 to live on. That was a lot more than she could make with her bachelor's degree, and she would be doing the work she had dreamed she would do when she was in junior high. So she attended Major State University, which offered good day care, loans she could repay, and loan forgiveness if she had several years of lower earnings. Upon graduation she passed the bar examination and then worked for four years at a major law firm in San Francisco that had an in-office day-care facility before devoting more and more of her time to public-interest law.

RICH BLACK'S RULE #47.
Financial aid for graduate professional school consists predominantly of loans. Calculate your monthly income with the degree before you borrow for the education.

The Timeline and the Checklist

What	When	Done?
Begin taking the gateway courses for a major that will lead to graduate professional study in the discipline you want.	College freshman	
Work, volunteer, secure an internship or engage in some activity related to the profession to test your commitment and demonstrate your ability.	Anytime in college	
Take cram courses for the test for professional school and take the tests.	College junior or early senior year	
Apply for admission. Some graduate fellowship applications are due as early as mid-November. Contact the schools to which you will apply for admission and fellowships, get their application schedules, and follow them exactly.	October or November of senior year	
Complete the Free Application for Federal Student Aid listing all the institutions you are considering.	February of senior year	
Consider your offers. Note—Most graduate professional schools have waiting lists. You may be accepted to a more prestigious school late in the summer. Be alert to that possibility if you are on a waiting list.	Spring of senior year	
Complete loan forms and follow all other instructions from the school.	Summer before graduate study	

3

Robert

A part-time professional degree candidate
Typical of some students in education,
management, engineering, library science and
other professions

Robert and I got to talking about financing a graduate education on a plane from Atlanta to Dallas recently. I was impressed with how he had financed a part-time professional graduate degree using employer benefits, which supported his career development. When he was five years out of college, he had a job selling and installing security systems in Charlotte, North Carolina. He also had a pregnant wife, a son, two cars, car payments, and season tickets to the Charlotte Hornets. The work paid the bills, including his undergraduate student loans, but he could see that a more satisfying position would require more education. So what to do? Quit his job and borrow for the full-time degree? That was an option, but his grades had been merely respectable in college, and he didn't think he could get into one of the really high-powered professional degree programs. Plus, he would need to borrow a great deal to support his family. Should he assume his wife could support him while he went to school? Spousal support is a time-honored tradition in financing graduate education, and Bob's wife found her career rewarding and fulfilling. But with the second child on the way, she was cutting back to a part-time schedule for a few years, so her financial contribution to the family would be less, not more.

So how about keeping the job and studying part-time? Within

30 miles of their apartment he found part-time evening programs in business, management, engineering and law, and if he was willing to move, there was even a master's program that focused on the development and management of security systems. He considered going to work for one of the colleges in the area, which would then allow him to attend classes for up to six units for free, but after discussing his plans with his boss he decided he liked his present employer too much to explore that option.

His company would pay half of his tuition and fees as long as he passed the courses, and his boss said that he would give him three hours a week off with pay, and allow him to use three hours a week of paid vacation, on the condition that he remain with the company for a year after he completed the degree. He figured that he would take two courses a semester, which would give him 12 units each semester toward a 30-credit master's degree. At that rate it would take him two and a half years to complete a degree that would only take a year if he were to go full-time, but he could do the whole thing by borrowing less than $10,000, and that felt pretty good. In fact, he took three years to complete the degree, because in his second year he went down to one course during the spring semester because the Hornets were hot, but when they bombed in the playoffs he took two courses in summer school. He vowed he would never take two courses in summer school again because he did nothing but work, sleep, and study for eight weeks; his wife finally took their (by now) two children to her parents' condo on the Outer Banks because he had no time for them, and he still got a C in the finance course.

There are literally hundreds of thousands of part-time graduate students in America today, primarily in professions such as education, management, public administration, counseling and engineering, but also in some more academic degree programs as well. Many members of the military pursue graduate degrees part-time. These programs do take more time, but they integrate study and work while frequently being supported at least in part by employers. Further, the networking in these programs is excellent: your study partner may give you a line on your next job, or you may find just the person your company needs for a new project.

RICH BLACK'S RULE #48.
Part-time graduate study is an effective avenue toward a degree, greater job satisfaction, and greater job security for hundreds of thousands of Americans every year. Check it out. Get started!

The Timeline and the Checklist

What	When	Done?
Investigate part-time professional degree programs in your area of interest. What are the out-of-pocket costs of a part-time program? What loans or other financial aid are available to part-time students?	College senior or anytime in professional career	
Learn what educational benefits your employer offers.	Anytime in professional career	
Complete the admissions forms, any loan forms, forms your employer may want, and enroll in your first course. Tell your friends your social life is on hold till you get your degree.	When you are ready	

4

Lee

A candidate for a doctorate in chemistry
Typical of students in the sciences and engineering

I've been following Lee now for about ten years. When I first knew him, he was on my son's track team, and I've been impressed with his ability not just to leap over the academic hurdles in the race to his doctorate, but also to clear the financial hurdles as well. When my son was a sophomore he reported that the chemistry teacher had selected Lee as a teaching assistant. There he was at the spring open house demonstrating experiments: he really knew how the compounds interacted, and he planned his demonstrations carefully so the rest of us would understand as well. His mother was a real estate agent, his father an accountant, and neither could quite understand his passion for chemistry, but they both supported it. His undergraduate studies were pure joy because he got into a freshman seminar with a faculty member who gave him the same access to his labs that he extended to graduate students. He was well on his way to graduating with highest honors when he began to research graduate programs.

I hadn't realized how much thought could go into choosing a graduate program until I asked Lee about it all when he came to my son's annual Fourth of July picnic. First, as an undergraduate, he had deliberately done a research project for one of the strongest faculty members so he could ask advice on graduate chemistry programs and get a letter of recommendation. The professor not only came up with a list of the most outstanding chemistry departments—four Ivy League, one in Texas, one in North Carolina, three West Coast, one in Chicago and two Big Ten—he even arranged for several departments to pay Lee's way to campus for a visit. If a graduate program thinks you are really hot, it may pay for you to visit its campus. He took the Graduate Record Exams in the fall of his senior year, and had the admissions and fellowship applications completed by the end of October.

Some of the universities responded almost immediately with offers of a fellowship to cover tuition and fees, and a stipend for the remainder of his first-year expenses. These universities also indicated that there would be a strong possibility of a teaching assistantship and a fellowship in the second year and a research assistantship in the third and fourth. He could expect to take his qualifying exams at the end of the fourth year, and a dissertation fellowship would be offered for the fifth year. He would finish his doctorate in the fifth year, which is about as soon as it can be done, assuming that his research goes well. Finally, several of these institutions indicated that they had a good record in funding postdoctoral fellowships to support additional research and study after his doctorate.

He consulted with his major professor, who advised him to wait for offers from the University of Chicago and two of the Ivy League institutions. His undergraduate record was outstanding, and he might have the opportunity to study at one of them. Lee's experience is typical of students in chemistry, biology and many areas of engineering. Faculty can fund teaching assistants for instruction of undergraduate laboratory sections of courses, and research assistants for various research projects supported by grants from the federal government and private industry. The pathway to graduate study in engineering and the physical sciences is rigorous, including math and scientific education from high school, but for those who study at the graduate level, there is grant support that generally makes extensive borrowing unnecessary and allows students to obtain their doctorates in as little as five or six years. The next step is obtaining a faculty appointment at a major research university and getting tenure, but that's another topic for someone else's book.

RICH BLACK'S RULE #49.
Graduate study in the sciences and engineering is supported with fellowships and research assistantships. Few students borrow. Take the math and science courses to prepare for these challenging and rewarding careers.

The Timeline and the Checklist

What	When	Done?
Take as much math and science as you can schedule.	High school	
Participate in research projects or other activities with faculty contact.	College	
Take GRE cram course.	Late in college junior year	
Research graduate department to which you will apply. Do they have what you want? What is their time-to-degree? Can they provide adequate financial support?	Late in college junior year	
Take Graduate Record Exams.	Late in college junior year or early in senior year	
Complete admissions and fellowship applications.	Late in college junior year or early in senior year	
Complete FAFSA and need-based financial aid forms required by particular institution.	February of senior year	
Visit campuses and departments of colleges in which you are interested.	When support offered	

5

Margaret

A candidate for a doctorate in English
Typical of students in the humanities and social
sciences

Margaret had a way with words. While her friends let teen-age jargon like "cool," "tubular" and "totally awesome" creep into their freshman papers, her prose became precise. She began to write like the critics she studied. . . . "His style was entering its last phase: disjointed, arbitrary, surreal . . . " Sometimes the discussion sections of her literature survey courses became dialogues between the teaching assistant and herself. She was asked to present a paper on Emerson and Whitman at a conference on 19th-century American authors, and subsequently published her work. Plainly, this woman had a gift for the humanities. How did she plan her graduate career? She went to the career center and read the materials, but then she checked out what she had learned with the provost of our university, who had been chair of the history department, while both of them were walking back from a recruiting luncheon for prospective freshmen. The provost listed several characteristics of a strong program in the humanities and social sciences: close contact with professors, classes in how to teach for teaching assistants, clear understanding of time commitment for teaching assistants, a departmental graduate student association, multiyear fellowships or at least a clear path to the degree, easy availability of language courses and support for students who find difficulty with language requirements.

Like the students in the physical sciences, Margaret applied for fellowships and assistantships at universities that had outstanding departments in English. What she learned was that several of them would give her a fellowship in her first year, and gave promise of a teaching assistantship in the second year, but there were few opportunities for research assistantships. In other words, about the time she was making good progress toward completing her course work for her doctorate, she would have only teaching assistantships for support. The question was, could she get started soon enough on her dissertation so that she would need to borrow for only two or three years? Her university even had a special fellowship for the year in which she would complete her dissertation, but the problem was the gap in between.

Margaret's experience is typical of doctoral students in the humanities and the social sciences. Some fellowship support is available for outstanding students, but it rarely extends throughout the entire time of graduate study; usually ample teaching assistantships are offered, because many discussion sections for undergraduates have to be taught in the large survey courses. If your own department doesn't have a teaching assistantship open, check related departments. The statistics department may hire graduate students from mathematics; the comparative literature department may hire graduate students from German; and agricultural resources may hire economics students. But a doctorate in the humanities or social sciences sometimes takes five years of course work before the qualifying examinations for the dissertation. Then the problem is to collect the data and get the dissertation completed. All too often the language examinations remain to be passed. And it is here that a doctoral student can become stymied. Too frequently ABD (All But Dissertation) students obtain full-time employment outside the university with the notion of supporting themselves while they complete their research, and somehow the research is never completed. So be sure to check if the department has dissertation-year fellowships. These are another mark of a strong department and a good graduate program. Students frequently resort to loan support, and that is appropriate, as long as the total amount borrowed can be repaid by the anticipated income.

RICH BLACK'S RULE #50.
Fellowships and teaching assistantships do support doctoral candidates in the humanities. Finish that degree as quickly as possible to minimize loan debt.

The Timeline and the Checklist

What	When	Done?
Take Graduate Record Exams. Complete admissions and fellowship applications.	Junior or early senior year	
Visit campuses, talk with major professors, check out graduate student associations, research and teaching assistantship opportunities in related departments.	Junior or early senior year	
Review extramural fellowship directories located at graduate division office, career center, or library.	Junior or early senior year	
Complete FAFSA and need-based financial aid forms required by particular institution.	February of senior year	

Appendix

New Loan Repayment Options

Students will have the opportunity to borrow under the Federal Family Educational Loan Programs (Federal Stafford Loan Program, Unsubsidized Federal Stafford Loan Program, Federal Parent Loan for Undergraduate Students) or the Ford Direct Student Loan Programs (Ford Direct Loan Program, Ford Direct Unsubsidized Loan Program, Ford Direct Parent Loan Program), depending on which set of loans is offered at their college or university. The interest, deferments and other terms of these loan programs are similar, but the length and conditions of the repayment can be different.

The Federal Family Education Loans (FFEL) are repaid over 10 years; at present their interest rate is less than 8%, and therefore I recommend a rule of thumb of $13 a month per thousand dollars borrowed. According to the newsletter of the National Association of Student Financial Aid Administrators in July 1994, the Direct Loan Program has four different repayment options: the Standard Repayment Plan, the Extended Repayment Plan, the Graduated Repayment Plan, and the Income-Contingent Repayment Plan. Let's look at each of these plans to understand their advantages and disadvantages. When we have reviewed Direct Loan repayment options, we can look at how similar results can be achieved with the Federal Family Education Loans.

The Standard Repayment Plan

This is the same repayment plan that lenders have used for years. You can use the $13-a-month-per-thousand-dollars rule. The advantages of this plan are that your payments end 10 years after they start, which sounds like a long time to a person in their 20's, but isn't so long after all when you get to your late 30's. The disadvantage of this plan is that your payments can consume a major part of your starting salary.

The Extended Repayment Plan

This plan lets you stretch your payments out to 12 years if you have borrowed less than $10,000 and extend them to 30 years if you have borrowed more than $60,000. The advantage of the Extended Repayment Plan is that your payments are lower than they would be under the Standard Repayment Plan. The disadvantage of it is that you will still be making your loan payments at 55 when your kids are in college. Let's say you borrow $10,000 at 8%. (As I write the interest rate is lower, 6.25%, but rates are headed up.) If you take the standard plan, your payments will be $121 a month for 10 years, and with the extended plan, $108 a month for 12 years. No big deal either way. But now, let's take the $60,000 debt. Over 10 years the payments will be $728 a month; over 30 years they will be $440 a month. My first observation is, don't borrow $60,000 unless you are headed for a remunerative profession like medicine, management, or corporate law. My second observation is that while it is an advantage to make those lower payments early in your career, it is a major disadvantage to make them for 30 years. Can't decide on the tradeoffs? Read on; the friendly feds make it more interesting.

THE GRADUATED REPAYMENT PLAN

This plan takes the Extended Repayment Plan, cuts the payments early in the repayment period and increases them at the end. For the $10,000 loan, therefore, the initial payment might be $70 and the final payments $180 over the 10-year life of a loan. For the $60,000 debt, the initial payment might be $220 and the final payments $660. The advantages of this approach are that payments are lower early in the repayment period, when presumably borrowers' incomes are more modest, and higher later when incomes are higher. The disadvantage of graduated repayments is that while incomes do rise in the course of a career, so do expenses. Borrowers tend to gather spouses, children, mortgages, and PTA dues as life goes along, and so it may be no easier to repay a loan later than sooner. Think carefully before you enter a graduated repayment loan program.

THE INCOME-CONTINGENT REPAYMENT PLAN

The idea behind this repayment plan is that people who make a little can only afford to repay a little of their loan, and people who make more can repay more of their loan. That makes sense, doesn't it? And so the people in Washington have come up with a repayment plan that can last for as long as 25 years, and if you haven't paid off the loan at the end of that time, the rest is forgiven. You give the Department of Education permission to look at your income tax forms for 25 years so they can figure your payments, and then just make your payments. If you don't make much, your payments are 3% of your income, and if you make a lot more, your payments can be up to 15% of your income. There is a slight reduction in your monthly payments for each dependent.

The Department of Education provides a table to estimate your repayments. Assume that you have borrowed $10,000 and you are going to earn $10,000 a year working through a temporary agency while you write poetry. Also assume you have no dependents.

Your monthly payment will be $48. Should you continue this practice for 25 years, your payments would never increase, and you never would pay off your loan. Incidentally, if you use the $13-a-month rule from the conventional 10-year repayment program, your payments would be $130 a month for 10 years. So the Income-Contingent Repayment Plan really helps out low-income persons who have borrowed for college.

Now assume that you have borrowed $10,000 and you are making $45,000. Your payments will be $218 a month, and you will repay the loan in about 4 years.

The Department of Education will explain these four plans to you before you go into repayment, and you can switch between them as long as you are not in default. Which one do I recommend? Well, that depends on your circumstances. If you have borrowed more than $10,000 and you expect to have a low income for many years, take the income-contingent program. If you have borrowed more than $10,000, are still in your 20's, and are starting on a career with rising earnings expectations, take the Standard Repayment Plan. You will have your loan paid off before the children and the other mid-life financial responsibilities—I almost said crises—come along. Graduated repayments look like an exercise in escalating pain to me. No sooner do you get the payments accommodated into your monthly budget than they increase again. I also do not recommend the extended plan, which strings out payments over 30 years. An education is one of life's major expenses, but only one. There is also the need to save for retirement, the need to purchase a house, and the expense of your children's college educations. When repayment of your own educational debt is added to meeting these needs, there will be little left for present expenses. We all need enough resources for the present.

This discussion has focused on repayment options for the Direct Student Loan Program. What do you do if you have a Stafford Loan and you want to stretch your payments out? You contact your loan servicer—the outfit that sends you your bills—and say that you want a consolidated loan with income-sensitive repayment terms. If you are current on your loan payments, or if you haven't entered repayment yet, you can consolidate Subsidized and Unsubsidized Stafford Loans into a single loan, and you can stretch the repayments out for 20 years. There are even graduated payment options if you want to explore those. Many lenders don't collect their own Stafford Loans; they sell them to investors who either contract for the collection of the loans or do it themselves. One of the largest investors is Sallie Mae, the Student Loan Marketing Association. Sallie Mae has an excellent reputation for customer service, as do many other loan servicing agencies, and will work with you to set up a loan billing schedule that will meet your needs. If all else fails, the federal government may make a Direct Loan to you to pay off your FFSLs, but that should not be necessary.

Summary of the Rules

RICH BLACK'S RULE #1.
Cost minus parent contribution minus student contribution equals need.

RICH BLACK'S RULE #2.
Most of the difference in the student's total cost of education is the cost of tuition. Costs for room and board are surprisingly uniform at public or private colleges.

RICH BLACK'S RULE #3.
Students can reduce total educational costs by as much as $3,600 if they live at home. Balance this savings against lost educational opportunities.

RICH BLACK'S RULE #4.
Recent changes in need analysis rules, particularly the exclusion of home equity, have made it easier for students to qualify for need-based financial aid.

RICH BLACK'S RULE #5.
Parents provide the parent contribution through some combination of monthly savings before college, monthly payments during college and loan payments after college.

RICH BLACK'S RULE #6.
Parent contribution is divided by the number of family members in postsecondary education. Get two for the price of one.

RICH BLACK'S RULE #7.
Student contributions are calculated from previous year's income in excess of $1,750 and 35% of student assets. A student with income in excess of $1,750 a year will reduce eligibility for aid.

RICH BLACK'S RULE #8.
Scholarships and grants are gift aid, which is the best kind of aid because it doesn't have to be earned or repaid.

RICH BLACK'S RULE #9.
Estimate your loan payments by rounding the total amount borrowed up to the nearest thousand. Multiply $13 by the number of thousands to determine your monthly payments. If your monthly payment is more than you can afford on what you expect to earn, then seek less costly education.

RICH BLACK'S RULE #10.
Most students can work up to 15 hours a week during the academic year without adversely affecting academic achievement.

RICH BLACK'S RULE # 11.
A financial aid package is a combination of scholarship, grant, loan and employment awards funded by the federal government, the state government, the colleges themselves and outside agencies.

RICH BLACK'S RULE #12.
Get the FAFSA and the other forms well before the deadline and complete them carefully, reading the instructions when you have any questions. Make copies of every form you mail, and file before every deadline.

RICH BLACK'S RULE #13.
Colleges meet financial need with a financial aid package, which is a combination of scholarship, grant, work and loan. Colleges differ in the amount of scholarship and grant in the package, so compare packages carefully.

RICH BLACK'S RULE #14.
All colleges will require tax forms and other supplemental documents from at least some of their applicants. Follow the instructions of the colleges to which you apply. Make copies of every form submitted and meet every deadline.

RICH BLACK'S RULE #15.
Be prepared for a succession of offer letters, understand the change that each represents, sign and return them as the instructions will provide, and appeal if you think it's appropriate.

RICH BLACK'S RULE #16.
File an appeal that is factual with supporting documentation. Use the college's appeal forms if any are appropriate.

RICH BLACK'S RULE #17.
Apply for financial aid each year. Assume that the financial aid will be somewhat different in the upperclass years, but adequate to support the student through to graduation.

RICH BLACK'S RULE #18.
40% of American college students can't be wrong. Financial aid—along with the student's own earnings—can make a college degree a reality. That degree will make you a better provider for your kids, and a better role model for them as well.

RICH BLACK'S RULE #19.
If you are a parent, the federal government does not expect your parents to make a contribution toward your education to determine your need for financial aid.

RICH BLACK'S RULE #20.
Don't default, but if you do, negotiate with your student loan billing agency and resume regular payments. Defaulters lose eligibility for all financial aid, not just loans.

RICH BLACK'S RULE #21.
Application deadlines are set with high-school seniors in mind. But parent students who meet the deadlines can give themselves substantial financial benefits.

RICH BLACK'S RULE #22.
Child care can be included in the parent student's budget, but often only after filing a separate appeal.

RICH BLACK'S RULE #23.
Parent students can calculate expenses and resources thousands of dollars higher or lower than financial aid officers because they have different assumptions. Therefore, look at the financial aid offer letter, then make your own statement of expenses and financial aid. Compare the two and make your decision.

RICH BLACK'S RULE #24.
If you are a parent, and you and your spouse had a total income of less than $12,000 in the previous year, your student contribution is zero.

RICH BLACK'S RULE #25.
Don't forget to ask mom and dad. They might chip in.

RICH BLACK'S RULE #26.
Public assistance can provide support, particularly for the parent student's dependents. Check it out: you may be able to attend college and increase your employability if you or your children are supported.

RICH BLACK'S RULE #27.
VA benefits are a solid foundation to which other financial aid programs can be added to pay for a college education.

RICH BLACK'S RULE #28.
Your student contribution is the amount you are expected to provide, probably from a student job, if you and a spouse made more than $12,000 in the prior calendar year. If you cease working, you can appeal once the academic year begins.

RICH BLACK'S RULE #29.
Loans can be a good investment for parent students. Figure the loan repayments. If they are less than the additional amount you can make with the college degree, go ahead and take the loan.

RICH BLACK'S RULE #30.
Employer education benefits are a great way to pay for undergraduate degrees. Find out what your employer's rules are and take advantage of them.

RICH BLACK'S RULE #31.
Two students who are married have two financial aid packages. It's possible for a married couple to finance a postsecondary education.

RICH BLACK'S RULE #32.
If you're a parent student with a spouse who can support you and your children, then your out-of-pocket expenses for college will be much lower than your calculated financial aid budget. You may be able to overlook the student contribution, and easily earn and borrow enough for your college education.

RICH BLACK'S RULE #33.
Family contribution is divided by the number of family members who are at least half-time students for at least one term. It's economical to have parents and children in college at the same time.

RICH BLACK'S RULE #34.
If your child has academic achievement and leadership potential and is physically, mentally and medically qualified, encourage him or her to consider the service academies because they are a fully subsidized educational opportunity.

RICH BLACK'S RULE #35.
The military services offer a series of financial aid opportunities for higher education. If military life appeals to you, check out the opportunities the military services offer.

RICH BLACK'S RULE #36.
The Americorps program has ancillary benefits that finance education. That program and public service programs sponsored by nongovernmental agencies provide magnificent opportunities for service and self-discovery.

RICH BLACK'S RULE #37.
A full athletic scholarship covers almost all of a student's expenses. Lesser scholarships can still cover substantial amounts. Athletes will still need parental assistance, some work or loan to meet the balance of college expenses.

RICH BLACK'S RULE #38.
Division I athletics are highly competitive. Division III is intercollegiate athletics for personal development and the thrill of competition. Division II is somewhere in between.

RICH BLACK'S RULE #39.
Foster their dreams, but make them hit the books.

RICH BLACK'S RULE #40.
There are special financial assistance programs for students with disabilities. Check them out on a program-by-program basis.

RICH BLACKS RULE #41.
Make the effort! Apply for all the special scholarships for which you are eligible. But expect that you will have to apply for the regular financial aid programs as well.

RICH BLACK'S RULE #42.
There are rip-off search services and conscientious organizations. In general, if you want to pay a service, use the ones that advertise a large database against which the service matches the student. Beware of a search service that guarantees extravagant success.

RICH BLACK'S RULE #43.
In some circumstances financial aid officers can exercise "professional judgement" to increase student need, but they require clear documentation for the auditors.

RICH BLACK'S RULE #44.
For federal financial aid, graduate students are independent and no parent contribution is expected. Some professional schools ask for parental information to award grant funds.

RICH BLACK'S RULE #45.
Survey the programs available to you. Determine your career goals, academic achievements, time and energy. Then go for that graduate degree. There's a way to finance it.

RICH BLACK'S RULE #46.
Understand the different graduate level vocabulary so you know how much the graduate school or department will give you, how much you have to work, and how much you have to borrow. Be sure that you can repay your loans on what you are going to earn.

RICH BLACK'S RULE #47.
Financial aid for graduate professional school consists predominantly of loans. Calculate your monthly income with the degree before you borrow for the education.

RICH BLACK'S RULE #48.
Part-time graduate study is an effective avenue toward a degree, greater job satisfaction, and greater job security for hundreds of thousands of Americans every year. Check it out. Get started!

RICH BLACK'S RULE #49.
Graduate study in the sciences and engineering is supported with fellowships and research assistantships. Few students borrow. Take the math and science courses to prepare for these challenging and rewarding careers.

RICH BLACK'S RULE #50.
Fellowships and teaching assistantships do support doctoral candidates in the humanities. Finish that degree as quickly as possible to minimize loan debt.

Topical Index